Dr. Saba Hasanie

UNFOLDING

How biographical inquiry informs meaning-making in coaching psychology

Publisher's Note

Every possible effort has been made to ensure that the information contained in this book is accurate at the time of going to press, and the publishers and authors cannot accept responsibility for any errors or omissions, however caused.

No responsibility for loss or damage occasioned to any person acting, or refraining from action, as a result of the material in this publication can be accepted by the editor, the publisher, or the author.

First edition published in the United Kingdom in 2024 by Ideas for Leaders Publishing, a business of IEDP Ideas for Leaders Ltd.

Apart from any fair dealing for the purposes of research or private study, or criticism or review, as permitted under the Copyright, Design and Patents Act 1988, this publication may only be reproduced, stored or transmitted, in any form or by any means, with the prior permission in writing of the publishers. Enquiries concerning reproduction should be sent to the publishers at the following address:

Ideas for Leaders Publishing
42 Moray Place
Edinburgh
EH3 6BT
www.ideasforleaders.com
info@ideasforleaders.com

ISBN
978-1-915529-28-2 – Paperback
978-1-915529-29-9 – E-book

Your journey is still revealing layers of complexity that wonder and amaze me. To my original power structures Dr. Syed Abbas-Hasanie and Uroos Hasanie. Your wisdom is with me everyday.

Thank you to my best teachers and the greatest loves of my life - Saleh, Alyna and Arianna.

And finally thank you to my mentor and friend, without you this work would never exist. You are deeply missed Paul Brown.

I would like express my deep gratitude to all those who contributed to this research and its ongoing development and growth in practitioners and content. To the interviewees of this research, thank you for your wisdom. To my advisor Dr Pauline Armsby, thank you for your guidance during the doctoral process. And to my coaching colleagues who have helped me develop and expand the training programs, corporate applications and research foundations, thank you for your passion and support.

I would like to thank Roddy Millar and *Ideas for Leaders* for creating a platform for academic research to reach wider audiences. And thank you to Chris Murray for his expert editing of my research and writing.

This book is based on the research from the author's doctoral thesis, submitted to Middlesex University in 2022 as part of the requirements for the degree of Doctorate in Professional Studies. The thesis was entitled, *Biographical Dimensions of Meaning Making in Coaching Psychology: A critical evaluation of the use of biographical inquiry in the exploration of meaning making in coaching psychology.*

CONTENTS

Chapter 1
The Non-Conscious at the Intersection of Past, Present, and Future 15

Chapter 2
Why Clients Do What They Do 31

Chapter 3
The Study 61

Chapter 4
Expanding the Nature of Coaching: A Third-Generation Perspective 79

Chapter 5
The Rationale for Biographical Inquiry 103

Chapter 6
The Six Dimensions of Biographical Inquiry 121

Chapter 7
What Biographical Inquiry Tells Us 177

Chapter 8
Conclusions 203

Further Reading 215

Foreword

By Annette Fillery-Travis

Nearly twenty years ago, when I co-authored The Case for Coaching (Jarvis, Lane, and Fillery-Travis, CIPD 2006), a prevailing belief of coaching practitioners was that coaching should remain future-focused, leaving exploration of the past experiences of our clients to psychotherapy and similar fields. However, as coaching and psychotherapy have evolved and intersected over the years, this distinction has softened, allowing practitioners in each field to benefit from the other's research, practice, and insights.

Today, experienced coaches recognize the importance of helping clients make meaning of their experiences within coaching conversations, guiding them as they navigate hopes, fears, and self-doubt to reshape their identity and future. Yet, there remains a lack of frameworks that support practitioners in exploring this terrain—its dimensions, depth, and evidence-based foundations.

This book, supported by extensive research, addresses this gap by offering a guide for coaches on the biographical exploration of meaning-making. It situates readers within the research context, showing how this work intersects with narrative coaching, cognitive-developmental approaches, and similar perspectives. The research itself was conducted with senior practitioners operating at an epistemic level i.e. those experienced enough to transcend standard models and innovate within practice in response to client needs. Through extensive interviews the research draws specifically on their experience with biographical inquiry. The analysis of these interviews reveals a truly shared experience of the use of such inquiries, the impact of this approach and demonstrating its contribution to helping clients make meaningful changes.

While the research could have stopped there, the author goes further by integrating these findings with established research in coaching, psychology, and coaching psychology to present a framework for biographical inquiries. This framework offers significant benefits, enabling coaches and clients to collaborate more fully in the coaching process. It empowers clients to understand themselves more deeply, exploring the origins of their behaviours, beliefs, values, and identity. This depth makes change not only achievable but consistent and meaningful. Such an approach fosters ongoing development that is organic rather than rigidly staged or structured.

However, attention to ethics and professional practice is essential. Can coaches without psychological training conduct such inquiries safely? The author argues compellingly that, as the saying goes, "the cat is out of the bag": coaches increasingly recognize the relevance of clients' past experiences, and these conversations are becoming part of the coaching process. It is, therefore, preferable to provide a framework to structure this work in a safe, meaningful way.

I join the author in advocating for a shift in perspective among professional bodies, moving away from a tick box approach to the attainment of skills and competencies towards a more holistic and robust assessment of a coherent, evidence-based professional practice that meets the clients' specific needs. Such an approach is well established in professions as divergent as chemistry, law and consulting where the acquisition of mastery or chartered status is acknowledged in practitioners who have evolved their practice and approach to problems based on client experience and feedback. Such growth in shared research and practice will naturally expand the knowledge base within the field and foster innovative practice. Professional bodies are then able to fully serve their communities as forums for peer-reviewed knowledge and shared practice. This research by Dr Hasanie is an excellent example of such an approach. It developed through the experience of a seasoned practitioner and provides not only the context of the issue but also the evidence to address it and develop the field further.

I hope you enjoy this book as much as I have done, take the opportunity to change practice and consider researching your own professional interests.

Professor Emeritus Annette Fillery-Travis

Author's Note

The drive to create this book was born from two places. The first was the lack of research available in coaching psychology on working with childhood and family of origin data. The second, was an ethical pull to contribute to the growing yet still severely underdeveloped empirical research in coaching. Coaching Practitioners are needed in the research sphere more than ever before. As a field that has grown entirely through application versus theoretical foundations - our ability to advance as a field of professional practice needs more of its experienced practitioners to build the collective knowledge base.

The goal of this book is:

1. to present the research from my doctorate on the first evidence based framework for working with childhood data in coaching and how it relates to leadership tendencies in organizational life.
2. to use this research to build on the empirical evidence base in coaching psychology.

This book is intended for coaches and leadership development professionals who are interested in understanding the theoretical and research foundations of working with childhood data in coaching and how that impacts leadership tendencies.

Terminology Used in the Book:

- I use 'coach' as a generic term for all those who practice 'executive coaching';
- I refer to those who are being coached as 'the client' or 'clients';
- and those who I interviewed for my doctoral research as 'interviewees', all of whom are deeply experienced executive coaches who collectively represent the equivalent of over 200 years of wisdom. I have directly quoted many of their insights within the body of the text which we highlight with italics, with the hope you are as moved by their words and eloquence of inisght as I was when interviewing them.

This research has grown significantly since its inception. Now you can access various products related to this research that includes a certification and other programs targeted for coaches, programs designed for application in organizations, and further publications related to the topic. For further information:

https://globalosc.com/solutions/bdmm/

CHAPTER 1

The Non-Conscious at the Intersection of Past, Present, and Future

Introduction

This book is the culmination of the more than five-and-a-half years spent completing my doctoral studies in coaching psychology. However, it also represents the evolving nature of the industry of coaching as a whole and how we define the work of coaching within organizations. My starting point of this doctorate began after 20 years of working with people on a single idea that was simple but often unattainable in its execution: sustainable behaviour change. What I had known intuitively was that our personal histories played a major role in the way we showed up in organizational life. I searched for training programs, books, and research around how to meaningfully work with a client's past, but found little that directly applied to coaching. I found temporary supplements through training in psychology, psychotherapy, and counselling, and tried to adapt this training to my world, but was always left bewildered that we had nothing significant of our own in the field of coaching. This is when I began my doctoral journey and realized that the secondary research on this topic was almost non-existent in coaching, which set me on a path to not only build the empirical knowledge base in coaching on working with a client's past, but to train other coaches on what I had learned.

In this book, I will outline the vast journey of those academic years–taking you step-by-step through what was discovered in the secondary research, how I designed my research study, and ultimately the development of the most significant outcomes of my research. I will share with you references from the secondary research, but also direct quotes from the interviewees who represented more than 225 years of collective coaching wisdom that informed the creation of the following outcomes:

- The first evidence-based interdisciplinary coaching framework for biographical inquiry (BI) (e.g., working with a client's past) called the Biographical Dimensions of Meaning Making© (BDMM).
- An expansion of the definition and nature of coaching within a third-generation perspective in coaching psychology.
- Working with the non-conscious in coaching through the intersection of the past, present, and future.

This book begins with this last outcome, the intersection of the past, present, and future and how it informs the pivotal work we do in coaching. To me, this sets the tone for a very different way of looking at the work of coaching and therefore became the only option as a place to start.

This research began by looking at BI from the past as a way of trying to make sense of behaviours in the present. To inform why we do what we do, and equally importantly, what might get in our way of sustainably changing in the future. This exploration best exists not as one-way storytelling from client to coach, but rather as an exchange and interaction between client and coach. As the research reveals, BI is not a static process. It is not the equivalent of coaching-through-storytelling like leafing through an old photo album and then talking about the photos. Indeed, the past changes as the client and coach access these narratives together, exploring their meaning and how that meaning impacts the client's agency in the present and the hope of change they aspire to in the future.

What became apparent through the research was this constant intersection of time. How the past impacts the present. How the present is filtered by the past and the hope for the future. And how the future is a perspective that filters the reality in the present and the interpretation of the past. What was also being revealed was that this intersection of time was occurring in the non-conscious of the client. It was not until an explicit BI into the client's past was made that the client and coach together were able to bring something into consciousness. This chapter describes the dynamics of the three interlocking time dimensions, and the framework of the intersection of past, present, and future (the IPPF framework) that ultimately emerges.

The Intersection of Time between Past, Present, and Future

The concept of the intersection of time between past, present, and future first emerged after an interviewee noted, *'Can we as coaches work in a single time horizon?'* By the end of the interview, the answer was a clear 'No'. This concept was further explored by several interviewees subsequently, who described their varying experiences with how time dimensions seemed to be constantly intersecting. As one interviewee explained in particularly eloquent terms, *'We are accessing the past, present, and future all the time. A whisper from the future, the echoes from the past interact with this growing edge in a number of different ways in today'*. Another interviewee said, *'I think there's always a time factor to it. How do I make sense of the past, how it informs my current situation, but also what I want to do in the future and what's meaningful?'*

One interviewee succinctly summarized

the full scope of the intersection between past, present, and future, as follows:

> *"We're trying to integrate data in different time dimensions. I'm using it [BI] as a gateway to get them to access deeper reflections from the past, creating intentional dialogue around what's meaningful about that for them today, and how this all fits in a bigger perspective of future versions of themselves".*

When examining the secondary research available, there was very little available on the intersection of time in coaching. One academic, Reinhard Stelter, a professor of coaching psychology at the University of Copenhagen, whose research will be discussed several times throughout this book, did suggest that coaches should strive to help clients integrate events from the past and present within the perspective of the future in order to uncover uplifting insights and guidance (Stelter, 2014). However, Stelter's research did not recognize or address the interlocking nature of all three time horizons simultaneously. This chapter explores this interlocking nature of past, present, and future by first showing how the past interacts with the present. I will then explore how the present is a construct of the past and a projection of the future. Finally, I will offer a simple framework that examines this complex interaction of time dimensions.

The Past Is Forever Being Changed by the Present

"It's like looking into their past is able to give the client an understanding of where 'it' comes from; there is a sense of excitement already being able to feel into this new space, and then the need for action just comes. That is where the dance of coaching really begins".

Expert from Interview

More than half the interviewees acknowledged that engaging with BI into stories from the client's past was actually changing the client's experience of those past events. This happens because the client's present self is involved and interacting with the past during the storytelling. Put another way, as the coach is listening to the recounting of an event, that event has already changed from the actual experience the client had of it. The very act of looking at the past through the eyes of the present changes the history in some way, is a concept that has been explored and recognized in the secondary research on narrative practice (Pillemer et al., 1991; Pillemer, 1998, 2001;

Rubin et al., 1998; Habermas, 2011; Graci and Fivush, 2017).

The way the present changes the past–or at least, the client's experience of the past–was brought to life when one interviewee described how a client was relaying some part of their past and began to tear up. The emotional response sparked by the telling of this story was unexpected for the client. As the client explained to the interviewee, she had known that story for 40 years. But, for some reason, on that particular day during the coaching session, her soul was touched differently. *'It was like a doorway into something a little bit deeper than she had ever seen before was opened, and it could have only been opened in that present moment'*, said the interviewee. This experience exemplifies the essence of the idea that the past is forever being changed by the present. If this moment between client and coach had not taken place, exactly as it did in that present moment, the insight that the client experienced about the past could never have materialized.

Throughout the research, other interviewees described this same phenomenon in different words, such as *'reprocessing of old narratives'*, *'seeing the past for the first time'*, *'new insights just clicked'*, and *'something has changed in the room'*. All these comments point to the same

The Intersection of Past, Present, and Future

conclusion: when examined through the eyes of the present, the past materially shifts.

This insight led to the belief that the past will never define the client, because its meaning will constantly be changing alongside the client. It gives hope to the idea that no one is defined by their past. That the past is simply a way for the present to make sense of the things that happened to them once upon a time. What it also means is that healing and integration from past wounds and trauma is a constant possibility. The past does not exist as a static constant, but rather a series of events whose meaning changes as we change.

The materiality of this research outcome of the past being there to help inform the meaning-making happening in the present is a significant bifurcation in the field of coaching. Traditionally viewed as a field that focuses entirely on the present and the future, this insight directly contradicts the often artificial division made in coaching that our work should never go into the client's past.

The Present Is a Construct of the Past and a Projection of the Future

"I feel that when a person crosses an edge from a present state to another state, past or future, there is a delicate touch that they need to be left alone to do work between states, to truly cross that edge to something new".

Expert from Interview

The previous section examined how the past is constantly being changed by the present. Equally, the act of simply being in the present suggests the referential space of the past and the future exists simultaneously. Let's outline this with an example. The use of goal-setting is a common tool used in coaching. These goals, often set by the client in the present moment, are typically informed by past behaviours they wish to shift and likely aspirational targets they hope to achieve in the future. Coaching is a future-orientated field that requires examination of what is happening in the present context for the client. However, this present context is inevitably informed by the past as a reference point of what has worked and what has not worked. Therefore, any sense that a coach may have that the past has no place in coaching is likely failing to see that the past is already in the room. It is this foundational aspect of the past always being in the room that makes the complete avoidance of tools to help coaches navigate the past a major oversight in the field of coaching.

Another way to explore this notion is that the past represents our lived experience, and is therefore the only referential aspect the client has and therefore requires consideration. The future is a hope or an expectation of what could be. It is foundationally the whole purpose of coaching to explore how this expectation can be attained. This makes the present a place for experimentation, exploration, and integration. The present is a place where the past can take on new meaning, where the future can take on new hope, and the present is the dance floor that makes this all happen.

This 'intersection of past, present, and future'–a phrase and framework that emerged from the analysis stage of my research –was evoked in different terms by nearly a third of the interviewees. *'By examining our historical imprints, it's like we used the past to inform a more whole future',* said one interviewee. Another said *'Our body knows, you can feel it like guideposts that something has changed in the way they think about the past and future'.*

One interviewee even suggested that she begins in the future, before heading into the past:

> *"I invite visualizations of the future. What resources does the client need to enable confidence in going into the past. That's where the magic starts to happen. Many call it really spiritual. This is awakening the non-consciousness of multiple time dimensions".*

How the Non-conscious Emerges from the Intersectionality of Time

By looking at coaching as the intersection of the past, present, and future, or in others' words, an exploration of the lived experience (past) with expectation (future) and experimentation (present), you can see how much of this work can exist in the non-conscious realms of the client. Most of us move through life with our stories within us but seldom revisit them. It is as though our experience of living them was the first, and often only, interaction we had with them–like a movie we watched once. And while we may remember them, we seldom actively interact with them ever again. But the truth is our stories are so much more than simply memories of our life. They are the source code for why we do the things we do. They are the experiences that drive our patterns of behaviours. They define how we perceive and see the world. They are the source data for our biases, our passions, and our ways of loving and being loved. They drive so much of how we operate in the world; and for the most part, they remain in the past, safely stored as a part of us, but somehow distinct from us. It is only when we want to change–when the current way of operating in the world no longer makes sense or is no longer giving us what we need, or we hold a bigger expectation for ourselves, that we finally interrupt this autopilot of life and initiate the curiosity of how to make this change possible.

As coaches, the success of the experimentations you partner with your clients on needs to be informed by the experiences the client already has that might get in the way. In order for a client to truly experiment in the present with these notions of possibility, they will need to navigate certain past experiences, which sit in this non-conscious part of us, to see how they may be blocking the new possibilities.

Let's take, for example, a client who has the goal of working on their public speaking skills. While an exploration of the various ways the client can experiment with different ways of being in the present can be useful, inevitably the client will hit a block. Why? Likely, because at some point in their past the client developed a view on who they were in this capacity of public speaking, and this view feels fixed. For some, it may have been compounding negative experiences over many years that resulted in a perspective of 'not being good enough'. Or maybe a single event created so much embarrassment or pain, it felt insurmountable. But now, in the present, for whatever reason, this person wants to change. All that history around public speaking, their fixed view of themselves, sits in the non-conscious. It is not until there is an intentional focus on this past can the client really begin to unravel the complex tapestry that makes up their ability to sustainably change on this aspect.

As such, I created this very simple but effective way to visualize the complex interplay of the past, present, and future when related to behavioral change. Figure 1.1 encapsulates these views in an Intersection of Past, Present, and Future (IPPF) framework.

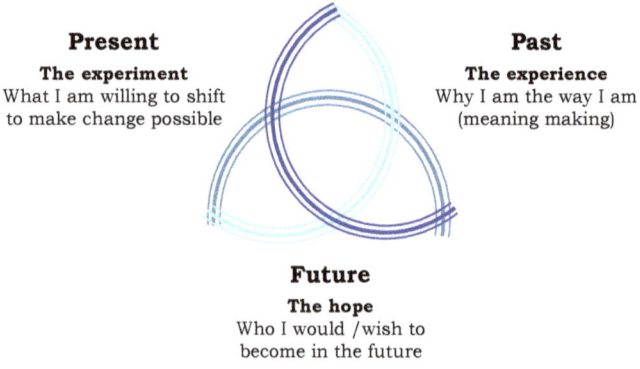

Present
The experiment
What I am willing to shift
to make change possible

Past
The experience
Why I am the way I am
(meaning making)

Future
The hope
Who I would /wish to
become in the future

Figure 1.1. The intersection of past, present, and future (IPPF)

Implications for Coaching

I started this book with the intersection of time outcome of my research because it fundamentally shifts how we view the work we do in coaching. By understanding that the past and future are always in the room with us when we coach, it makes the materiality of having tools to help us navigate this complex place of the past essential. A coach cannot work with a client without some consideration of all three time horizons. And as will be explored in later chapters in this book, looking at the past through BI is the key for discovering true meaning-making, the source code for why we do what we do. As such, the coach must be alert to moments of shifting meaning. When, for example, a client reflecting on some element of their past brings new awareness to the present that informs their future possibilities ... well this becomes what coaching is fundamentally all about: true sustainable behavioural change.

CHAPTER 2

Why Clients Do What They Do

Unfolding

This book presents a coaching-centric framework whereby coaches have a shared understanding of *why* their clients do what they do. This framework, which is the first empirically based coaching framework developed, focuses on a client's meaning-making structures, both at a conscious and a non-conscious level, through the use of biographical inquiry (BI). It shows how clients interpret their biographical data–their memories and events in their past–and then use those interpretations to influence their thinking and behaviours in the present. In short, the framework shows coaches how to explore why your clients do what they do through the exploration of their past.

The framework is called the *Biographical Dimensions of Meaning Making*© (BDMM) framework and is presented below.

FIGURE 2.1: The Biographical Dimensions of Meaning Making framework.

Biographical Dimensions of Meaning Making© (BDMM)

Emotional Spectrum

An exploration of the emotional capacity of the client over the full spectrum of escape to attachment emotions.

Hierarchy

An exploration of the evolving authority structure(s) in the client's life.

Peers

An exploration of peer-based dynamics including siblings, friends and the chosen family.

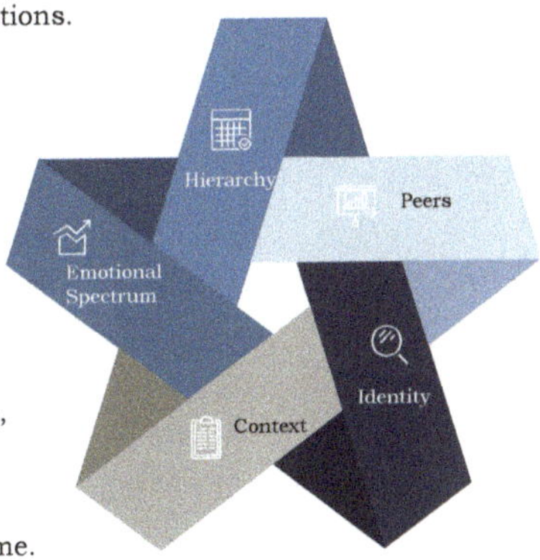

Context

An exploration of the socioeconomic, cultural and environmental influences on the client's life over time.

Identity

An exploration of the evolving sense of self from inherited to constructed identity.

Relationship

Encompassing the whole structure is the capacity to form and sustain relationships.

What Is Meaning Making?

Meaning making is the term used in psychology to describe why people act and think as they do. The precise definition of meaning making is as follows:

> Meaning making is the process by which we interpret situations or events in the light of our previous knowledge and experience.

The question addressed in this book is aptly described by one interviewee, how can coaches help their clients *'construe, understand, or make sense of life events, relationships, and the self?'*

The answer is found in *biographical inquiry*. BI is a process through which a coach and a client explore together the life history and experiences of the client, looking for the elements in the client's life history that influence–consciously or non-consciously–the client's present behaviour.

BDMM© is an evidence-based framework through which coaches can pragmatically apply BI in their coaching. This book describes the empirical research conducted, including an extensive review of past research in multiple disciplines, which led to the identification of six key dimensions of BI. BDMM© is thus the first empirically based model of working with the past in coaching.

The Origins of the Search for a Biographical Inquiry Framework

My own past and family history certainly influenced my quest for a practical framework for the use of BI in coaching.

Coaching was not my first career. I was in sales and marketing first, then human resources, and then management consulting. When I finally transitioned to executive coaching in 2010, I felt I had at last found my professional home. Since then, I have accumulated more than 10,000 executive coaching hours and worked with executives in more than 300 organizations.

The research at the heart of this book, consisting of interviews and waves of analysis, as well as a deep dive into the existing research in the coaching and psychology fields, is focused on executive coaches. All of the interviewees were experienced executive coaches, and it was their executive coaching experience that helped identify the key elements of a coaching model based on BI.

However, the catalyst of my research was my own insight into the influence of my biography on how I worked as an executive coach. In their seminal book, *Supervision in the Helping Professions*, Robin Shohet and Peter Hawkins suggested that those of us in the helping professions would tend to approach our work from our own pathologies. That was certainly the case for me. First, I am the daughter of first-generation immigrants to Canada–my father was an academic but experienced significant discrimination early in his career. My mother was catapulted into a society she did not understand nor felt connected to, and therefore turned to spirituality to anchor her life. My identity can be said to be multi-ethnic, multi-religious, and multi-cultural–an identity that has been the greatest source of both confusion and clarity in my life. In addition to this background, I further complicated the mix by choosing to become an executive coach in a country that was not my place of birth: Singapore. I was hypersensitized to my own meaning-making narratives and personal conflicts with identity, but also able to see this dilemma in others. Singapore is an extraordinary melting pot of people from all over the world.

In fact, to really understand Singapore you need to understand its history from the Crown colony of Singapore founded by the British in 1867, to its merger with Malaysia in 1963, to finally becoming an independent republic in 1965. The people of this country endured social unrest, racial tensions, and political divergence that ultimately gave rise to the diverse Singapore we know today. I feel that many of the people from this country and the millions of foreign talent drawn to its shores are all seeking something different–manifesting in a culture I had never experienced until the moment I moved here.

This unique context led me to work with clients on behaviour change by *first* understanding their background, their own sense of identity, their cultural history, and their relationships. In essence, I was trying to understand who they were through their past in order to help them in the achievement of where they are going for the future. I was integrating BI into my practice based on my own intuition of what was needed far before I realized the significant gap this approach ultimately identified in the coaching profession.

HASIE: A Pioneering Framework from Neuroscience

This informal application of BI became more formal when I began working with a framework from the field of applied neuroscience. Neuroscience involves research into how the brain works, and how such knowledge can be applied to help people. The framework in question, the Hierarchy - Attachment - Sibling - Identity - Emotional Tapestry (HASIE), was created by psychotherapist Dr Paul Brown. Brown developed

HASIE in the early 1970s when he was Director of Psychological Services for an executive career counselling firm in the UK. His goal was to create a guide for therapists that would then assess how a client's life experiences influenced the formation of the client's brain, including its neurochemistry and its neural circuitry response mechanisms.

Brown's framework focuses on five key dimensions of a person's biography:

Hierarchy: authority-based relationships in the client's life, beginning with parents.

Attachment: how the client as an adult creates and sustains relationships.

Sibling: the importance of peer groups (including siblings) in a client's life.

Identity: the complex interactions between the client's sense of self, social identity, and environmental context.

Emotional tapestry: how a client acknowledges and processes emotions.

I adopted the HASIE framework within my own practice and used it effectively with more than 50 clients over a three-year period. It was HASIE that cemented my support of BI as a coaching approach, as it was through its application that I began to get more structured data on the dimension of why we do what we do and where these patterns come from.

One fundamental insight I gained as I was applying HASIE in my coaching work was the *non-conscious* as well as conscious facet of meaning making. The non-conscious includes the pre-conscious, unconscious, sub-conscious or anything else that lies below the surface of human conscious awareness. It became clear to me that the non-conscious roots of meaning making were a vital function of BI. The past of my clients clearly influenced non-conscious patterns of behaviour occurring in the present.

Developing new insights on how the past was linked to non-conscious patterns of behaviours in the present was one of the catalysts of my decision to explore the evidence base around the use of BI. I was also encouraged by the consistently positive feedback from clients on the value of the biographical exploration in which we engaged. Finally, the patterns emerging from my work with my clients were evolving and expanding past the HASIE framework I was using.

With the support of my mentor, Dr Paul Brown, as the originator of the original HASIE model, I thus came to strongly believe that there was value and an unmet need in the coaching field for an evidence-based model of meaning making through BI specifically designed for coaching.

Unfolding

In order to fully understand the state of current thinking, my research led me to review all the secondary research available on the topics of meaning making, BI, and the non-conscious. As you can imagine, there needed to be some parameters in terms of how far and in what aspects of the research I wanted to go. The following sections highlight where choices were made to either include or exclude data, but perhaps even more importantly, what conclusions if any could be made regarding the three topic areas.

What you will discover from this section is that the information related to BI is seriously lacking in the research. There is a significant amount of tangential information but the holes in the empirical evidence base are evident. As you will discover through the subsequent chapters of this book, many of these holes will be addressed by the BDMM© framework.

Framing the Research

The first step was to consult and review any past academic research, also known as the research 'literature', that could help develop the intended framework.

The search for the empirical evidence to support a BI approach to coaching was guided by five research questions concerning meaning making, BI, and the non-conscious.

The first question was *whether meaning making needed to be identified for coaching to lead to high-quality and sustainability behavioural change* in the client. In other words, did the past impact present behaviour and how?

The second question to be explored was: *How does a client make meaning at a conscious and non-conscious level?* It quickly became apparent that in the context of meaning making, consciousness and non-consciousness are engaged in a constantly moving dance. Experiences are not necessarily stored in one or the other. The question, therefore, was: How can both consciousness and non-consciousness be used simultaneously in coaching?

The final three questions that framed the research related to BI. First, *was there evidence that BI was a useful approach to examine meaning making?* In other words, was exploring the history of a client a useful source for discerning the client's meaning making and did it provide deep insights for the client? Second, *what were the core dimensions to be considered in a BI process?* The dimensions identified by Brown would prove to be an important starting point. And finally, *would the evidence show that BI actually helps the coach access deeper levels of meaning making?*

To explore the academic evidence related to these questions required reaching into multiple disciplines, beginning with coaching, of course, but quickly moving into the emerging field of coaching psychology–the domain where eventually the research fit best. Research from psychology and applied neurosciences was also an important source.

My research into existing research and theories thus covered three topics:

Meaning making-related research. The theoretical foundations of meaning making were found in the fields of coaching and psychology.

Biographical inquiry-related research. As we will see later in this chapter, surprisingly little BI-related research was available in the field of coaching. The field of psychology had more to offer, although this research also had its limitations.

Non-conscious-related research. Research of the non-conscious through various applied practice approaches in the fields of coaching and psychology were considered.

The results of the review of the academic literature described above are covered in the rest of this chapter.

EXISTING RESEARCH ON MEANING MAKING

Theoretical Foundations

In psychology, the roots of meaning making can be traced to the seminal (and famous) work of psychiatrist Viktor Frankl, who declared the primary motivation of every individual is to discover meaning in life (Frankl, 1946). In the late 1960s, meaning making started to be studied in the context of individual learning, which eventually led to the use of meaning making in *constructivist learning* theory.

According to this theory, the knowledge of individuals evolves as they experience new things and acquire new information, all of which is added to their current knowledge. This led to the constructivist approach to meaning making in psychology, that is, what we perceive, believe, and construct through our life experiences becomes our reality (Sexton, 1997).

Constructivist theory has many applications, but its application in the field of developmental psychology–the study of how people grow, change, and adapt throughout their lives–was the most relevant to my research.

Meaning Making through Narration

One of the key methods for meaning making developed in the field of coaching psychology is the use of narration. In a study by Vogel (2012), there are three broad approaches to the use of narrative practice in coaching: story as the task of coaching; story as the content of coaching; and story in the context of coaching. The primary focus is on the unravelling of the meaning-making structures a client holds, based on the stories they tell themselves from a lifetime of experiences.

In his research, Drake (2016), who has contributed significantly to the exploration of narration as the task and content of coaching, has suggested that structure, phases, the relationships and movements of character, and connections between narration and growth are pivotal areas of exploration in the narrative landscape. It is the act of storytelling that is the most revealing process of the experience.

In contrast, McAdams suggests that narrative is the identification of an individual's truth, logic, and identity (McAdams, 2018). Pushing this idea even further is Reinhard Stelter of the University of Copenhagen. Stelter argued that meaning making is the process of attributing value to experiences, interactions, or relationships. To make meaning, clients must be able to understand how they feel, think and act–an understanding that is achieved by telling stories about the experiences (Stelter, 2007). In other words, clients discover their meaning-making structures through the stories they tell themselves from a lifetime of experiences.

From a coaching perspective, the effective use of narratives depends on dialogue and collaboration between coach and client. While the client will bring in a certain self-perceived reality, the coach can offer a new perspective that invites the clients to see the world differently compared with their existing views (Stelter, 2014).

Meaning Making through Constructivism, Cognitive Developmental, and Adult Development

It was the psychological domains of human life, as explored in Erikson's psychosocial theory (1950) and Piaget's cognitive development approach (1971), that eventually gave birth to ego development theory. The idea was that the ego matured and evolved through the stages of a lifespan due to the continuous interactions between the inner self and the outer environment. Specifically, ego development theory proved to be particularly interesting. According to this theory, the ego matures and evolves through stages of the lifespan through the interaction between the inner self and the outer environment–a theory pioneered by Jane Loevinger, who created the Washington University Sentence Completion Test (WUSCT), an assessment that examines how meaning is derived from within the individual. Loevinger's work is foundational in projective testing around meaning making in psychology and psychotherapy. It also gave birth to many other bodies of research such as Susanne Cook-Greuter's (1985) use of the Leadership Maturity Profile and William Torbert's Seven Action Logics (Merron et al., 1987).

Related to this area is the seminal work of Kegan in the field of constructivist-developmental psychology. Kegan explores the idea that 'the *person* is more than an individual' (Kegan 1982), analyzing the relationship between the individual and the social and arguing that development is about the continual settling in and resettling of this interaction. Kegan uses the term *subject* to refer to things that people are 'subject to' but not necessarily consciously aware of and the term *object* to refer to things that people are aware of and can take control of. This subject-object orientation is further explored by other researchers including Berger (2012).

These cognitive–developmental approaches

to coaching can be controversial (Wilbur, 1999) because they can be used in coaching to influence the sequential stages of clients, beyond their naturally occurring meaning-making experiences. This can be dangerous and only creates the illusion of stretch and expansion versus dealing with the more immediate concerns being presented by the clients–a major limitation of this approach. With the lack of other data on their clients, coaches can make inappropriate choices on these clients' developmental capacities (Bachkirova, 2014).

Limitations of the Research Related to Meaning Making

Exploring meaning making using a narrative process (Stelter, 2007; McAdams, 2018; Vogel, 2012; Drake, 2016) or adult development theory (Lawrence, 2017; Eigel and Kuhnert, 2005; Strang and Kuhnert, 2009; Bachkirova, 2011, 2014) revealed some significant limitations in the research.

First, two weaknesses in the narrative's perspective emerged: the stories may be incomplete, and the interpretations of the stories are developed through the biased prism of the client. The narratives perspective assumes clients will be able to effectively share full and complete stories, when in fact people are more likely to have fragmented or incomplete memories of past events. Therefore, the interpretation of the story that clients have shared around specific aspects of their lives may in fact be incomplete, since the story itself might just be a slice of the actual experience. In addition, the progress and growth identified through narrative practice is based solely on the individual's narrow perception, without any systemic perspective or larger context. For these reasons, the narrative's perspective is limited in its application, which reinforced my conviction that some overall framework for a BI practice was needed.

The stages approach was also incomplete in terms of the impact of the past on the present. As applied in coaching, this approach maps how clients move from stage to stage during the course of their lives, but does not delve into the origins of each stage. The focus is on stage progression rather than stage understanding–that is, on moving forward from the past, and not on understanding how the past explains present behaviour.

Even more troublesome than this weakness was the fact that I found limited *evidence-based research* on effective outcomes from either the narratives or stages of growth approach to meaning making. In simple terms, where is the empirical proof that these approaches work?

For example, gaps were found in the search for evidence supporting the stages approach to an individual's development, especially for the later stages of life. While the early stages of an individual's development could be linked to poor leadership, there was little evidence linking the later stages–when the individual would have theoretically amassed the knowledge and experiences to be a better leader–to more effective leadership.

The significance of this lack of empirical proof was compounded by the fact that the theory development and practice of these approaches was totally Western-centric, with no indication whether the theories, methods, or tools could be applied to clients who were not white, wealthy, educated, and/or Western.

Existing Research on Biographical Inquiry

Paul Brown's seminal research in BI that led to his HASIE framework, which kick-started the search for an effective, applicable coaching framework for meaning making, has already been described. A review of the empirical research shows support for some of the biographical dimensions in HASIE only. Even more importantly, there was no research that specifically examined the links between the different dimensions.

Much of the research on the impact of the past on present behaviour relates to leadership theories. Different studies tied the biographical histories of leaders, and notably childhood experiences, to their effectiveness as leaders. This correlation, however, was not supported by serious evidence-based methodologies, nor did they offer a clear framework for effectively using biographical data for coaching.

Biographical Inquiry through Narrative Practice

The previous section discussed the strengths and weaknesses of relying on client stories for meaning making. This section focuses more specifically on stories as a source of biographical data that can be used to uncover events that might impact or influence how clients behave today and their capabilities to learn and grow. Past academic research highlighted two interesting facets of BI through narratives. The first is what is called *personal event memory,* which are memories of events that are pivotal in explaining the behaviour of an individual today. Stories about these pivotal events should be particularly valuable, but are they complete? Do they represent the totality of the experience that feeds the clients' meaning making?

Another issue that arises with BI is *temporal organization*–that is, how the events of a life are organized in the mind of the client. If before the age of three to five or six there are likely no recallable memories, the events that occurred in early childhood after these ages are given a great deal of weight by the client. Most stories offered by a client are going to relate to the ages of 10 to 30. Therefore, BI requires careful consideration of the stories offered, and whether the specificity and detail of a story relates to its importance. Childhood memories may be recalled with vivid detail but are these memories truly turning points that influenced the growth and development of the individual? These turning points or life transitions can be most revealing, which explains why they have been the focus of research in coaching psychology.

The Systemic Perspective

Another development in coaching psychology is the introduction of more systemic approaches, where the client is seen as part of a system. It is the role that a client plays in their original system, which is normally the family of origin, that lays the groundwork for future growth. Much of the research on family of origin, however, looks at issues of attachment, autonomy, or power structures that have been applied for therapeutic practices. Our topic is not therapy, however, therefore these applications are of less interest. What we will focus on (see chapter 6) is on family-of-origin data that can be explored by coaches.

For example, one tool called the family-of-origin scale suggests that *autonomy*, *intimacy*, and *emotional expression* can have an impact on adult behaviour, indicating that these are three dimensions that should be considered in BI. Indeed, these dimensions are reflected in the HASIE framework discussed above, and will be represented in the BDMM© framework described in this book.

Context-Related Factors

One consideration that has been raised in relation to BI by some researchers, and which was not used in the HASIE framework, is the role of *context*–specifically the context of diversity and cultural heritage not only for the client but the coach as well. Coaches have a responsibility to understand their own cultural heritage–which includes external cultural characteristics, as well as internal characteristics, such as values and basic assumptions or fundamental beliefs–before assisting other people.

There is, however, little research on how BI can

help uncover the cultural and gender assumptions a client has formed over a lifetime, or on how to address the problem of coaches bringing their own cultural and gender assumptions (usually from a white, Western perspective) to the process.

Limitations in Existing Biographical Inquiry Research

The existing research offers an incomplete view on the use of BI in coaching. The key limitation of the research boils down to four important facts.

First, coaching has relied almost exclusively on the use of narrative practice to explore biographical data. While narrative practice can help the coach understand how to interpret stories, it does not identify the key areas of exploration that coaches should pursue to acquire a more complete and comprehensive view of the client's biography and the significant aspects of overall meaning making.

Second, narrative practice relies on the discretion of the client of what is material, significant and/or recalled, which may not be reflective of the full experience of the past. The client's non-conscious decisions on personal event memory and its temporal organization can leave holes in the overall meaning making the client is holding, and it is within these holes that some of the most significant meaning making may be had.

Third, by contrast in psychology, there is research that explores individual dimensions of BI, such as family of origin and attachment theory, but ignores others almost completely, such as peers and context. In addition, how to interpret the data for non-clinical or non-therapeutic purposes but instead for use in coaching has been almost exclusively ignored.

And finally, there is no material research or empirical data on the link made between the different dimensions of a client's life and how that relates to leadership behaviours and tendencies. While the field of constructivism and developmental psychology have linked stages to leadership tendencies and behaviours, they have not empirically linked this data to the exploration of the client's past as a source of insight and integration.

Existing Research on the Non-Conscious

Given the vastness of the topic of the non-conscious—be it from a psychology, coaching, and/or coaching psychology perspective—some decisions to limit the topic had to be made. This section is focused on exploration of the discovery of the non-conscious through BI via the narrative process and how to effectively work with it in coaching.

Oakley and Halligan (2017) describe the two aspects of consciousness: the experience of consciousness and the content of consciousness, which includes thoughts, beliefs, intentions, sense of agency, memories and emotions. The content of the non-conscious are mental processes that are inaccessible to consciousness but still influence judgements, feelings, or behaviour.

The existing research discussed the content of the non-conscious through four key lenses: (1) emotion-centric approaches, (2) somatic experience, (3) narrative approach and (4) reflective practice.

The Non-Conscious Through Emotions

From a coaching psychology perspective, emotions and the non-conscious have long been linked. For example, coaches may be working with clients whose behaviours are driven by anxiety over a non-conscious threat, who have been taught as children never to show emotions, or who are transferring early-life emotional pain into the present (Roberts and Brunning, 2019). These emotional drivers sit below the surface, outside the immediate consciousness of the client.

Unfolding

In exploring the categorization of emotions, the London Protocol of Emotions, dividing emotions into *attachment* emotions (love/trust, excitement/joy) versus *escape* emotions (sadness, shame, disgust, anger, fear), and adding the 'potentiator' of startle/surprise, provides a useful mapping system of emotions to non-conscious behavioural patterns (Brown and Brown, 2012).

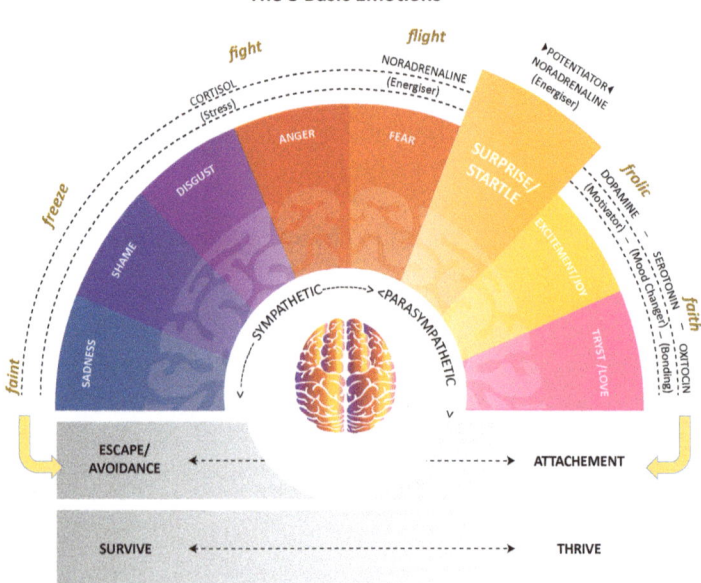

The London Protocol Of The Emotions
© ION Consulting International Pte Ltd 2023

The Non-Conscious Through Somatic Work

Somatic work relates to working with what the body rather than the conscious mind is telling us. In coaching, somatic work is a process of accessing and uncovering the non-conscious (Aquilina and Strozzi-Heckler, 2019).

According to R. Strozzi-Heckler's (2014) seminal book, *The Art of Somatic Coaching*, somatic coaching focuses on the body as a fundamental source of learning and change that enables the body to understand emotions and narratives over a lifetime (Aquilina and Strozzi-Heckler, 2019).

Coaching psychology research notes that a coach must be able to connect with their own body dialogue as it reflects any conscious or non-conscious insights that might be coming from the client (Grimley, 2019).

The Non-Conscious Through Narratives

There is a consensus among researchers in the field of narratives that the narrative practices allow access to the non-conscious. Vogel (2012) notes, for example, that while most of meaning making is happening non-consciously, the conscious mind is attempting, through narrative, to imbue these below-the-surface experiences with coherence and intent. As critics note, however, there is little evidence-based research showing cause-effect dynamics between narratives and the non-conscious. (Rutten and Flory, 2020).

Reflective/Reflexive Practice in the Non-Conscious

Reflective practice is a critical dimension in the shifting of the non-conscious into consciousness. Self-reflection is the starting point, but to be truly effective in surfacing the non-conscious, self-reflecting should involve a partner (Kempster and Iszatt-White 2013). This dynamic process of reflecting on lived experience, probed by another thinking partner, will create interpretive observations of what is really going on (Ellis et al., 2011).

Stelter (2007) describes the dynamic relationship between coach and client as a consciously looping reflective process. Through conversation, he writes, there is ongoing reflection and renewed understanding of self. The very essence of good coaching is to create this dynamic relationship of reflection and insight.

To offer insightful interpretations to clients, however, requires coaches to approach events from a different perspective. However, as one researcher notes, reflective partners often hold the same ideologies. Coaches must work hard to maintain a sceptical attitude about client narratives.

Limitations of Existing Research on Non-Conscious

The topic of the non-conscious is vast and complex. In exploring the non-conscious, we must be able to understand it on multiple levels: (1) does it exist? (2) how can we access it? (3) from where does it come from? (4) how does it link to behaviours we want to change or shift? and finally (5) how can we shift it to create sustained behavioural change?

Most of the research on this topic in coaching explores the area of how we can access it, how it links to behaviours, and how we can create shifts. Unfortunately, however, there are few, if any, evidence-based practitioner models of where, what, and how a coach engages in this deep exploration into a client's non-conscious. Emotion-driven approaches and somatic and narrative-based practices might be access points, but there is a lack of real evidence-based frameworks and specific areas of inquiry that can help coaches to explore the vast and complex psychology of their clients to actually unlock the source of reframing these patterns into sustainable change for the client.

Conclusion

This chapter reviewed some of the key themes that emerged in past research on issues related to meaning making, BI, and the non-conscious. It also identified some insights that would later be applied to the research study that led to the BDMM©. Mostly, however, the exploration into past research revealed gaps and weaknesses in many of the areas of inquiry.

The next chapter reviews my research study, which aimed to address knowledge gaps in meaning making, BI, and the non-conscious, and build the foundation for a practical, coaching-centric framework of meaning making through BI.

CHAPTER 3

The Study

As explained in Chapter 2, my research was focused on the creation of a framework for coaches to have a shared understanding of *why* their clients do what they do. This *why* is focused on the client's meaning-making structures, at both a conscious and non-conscious level, primarily through the use of biographical inquiry (BI). Explicitly, the aim, which was achieved, was to create a new theoretical framework for conscious and non-conscious meaning making using BI within coaching.

This chapter will focus entirely on how the research was designed, conducted, and then analyzed for insights.

Coaching is a dialogue-based voyage of discovery, and I knew that my research would require the same approach. For this research, therefore, I conducted primary, semi-structured interviews with 13 extensively qualified coaches and psychologists to gain consensus on what is meaning making, and how coaches can access it with clients.

Before each interview, I sent a pre-interview questionnaire to each interviewee up to 48 hours before their interview. The data from the pre-interview questionnaire was not analyzed until *after* the completion of all semi-structured interviews to avoid significantly influencing or directing the interview, or introducing researcher bias.

Once each interview was completed, it was transcribed and uploaded to the software platform NVivo, which was used to code the transcript. The purpose of the coding was to identify the different topic areas–called 'nodes'– mentioned or described by the interviewee. The coding yielded 14 nodes, such as BI, coaching profession, context, emotions, ethics, hierarchy, meaning making, and peers, that categorized the learnings from the interviews.

Reflections as Data

The transcribed and coded interviews and pre-interview questionnaires constituted two sources of data for my research. The third source of data were my ongoing reflections during the process. As illustrated below (see Figure 3.1), I carefully reviewed and reflected on the data at three points:

- after each interview (at which time I also reviewed the pre-interview questionnaires);
- after the interviews had been transcribed and uploaded to NVivo; and
- after the interviews had been coded.

The reflections had at first an important process role, which was to take the knowledge from one interview and use that knowledge to influence and refine the questions and exploration occurring in the next interview. This created a linear progression in which the quality of the questioning, listening, and exploration improved from interview to interview. In fact, the second-to-last interview was only 46 minutes long, yet the depth of exploration was as rich as in the much longer earlier interviews.

The reflections would take on an even more seminal role, however, as a source of overall ideation and integration of thoughts–and would thus become distinct data themselves. As shown later in this chapter, after analysis of the bottom-up interview data resulted in the development of seven family themes, it was the top-down reflections data that reduced those themes to three major themes: the use of BI in coaching (see chapters 5, 6 and 7); expanding the nature of coaching within a third-generation perspective (see chapter 4); and using the intersection of past, present, and future to explore the non-conscious in coaching (as described in the opening chapter).

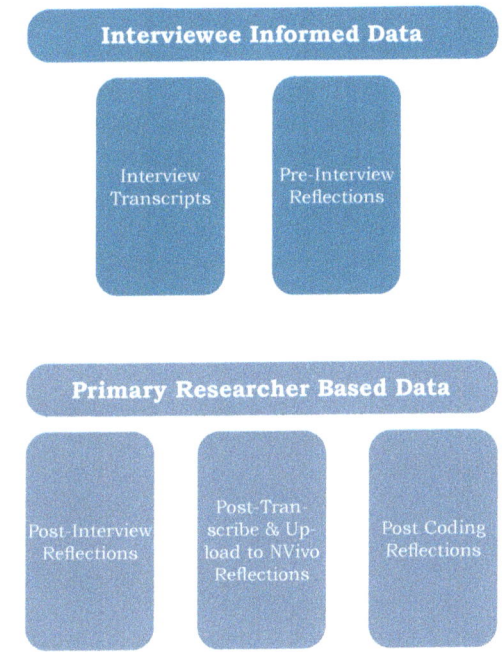

Figure 3.1 Data collection buckets and order of analysis

This research thus yielded five sets of data (two from the interviews, and three from me) collected in three stages. The data collected in the first stage consisted of the actual interview (1) and the post-interview reflections (2).

The second stage of data collection came once the interview was transcribed and uploaded to

NVivo (3). I would listen to the full interview from start to finish, cross-referring to the uploaded transcripts. I also read, for the first time, the pre-interview questionnaire (4) that had been sent to the interviewee and also uploaded to NVivo. I then reflected on what I had learned.

The third and final stage of data collection took place once all the data from the interview was coded in NVivo (5). I then reflected for a final time on what I learned from the interview, and the coding that emerged.

The analysis of these two buckets of data (interviewee data and my reflections) took place in four waves.

Wave 1

The first wave of analysis was the ongoing analysis done between interviews to inform the subsequent interviews. This level of analysis involved the original interview transcription and my notes and reflections on what was learned about (1) meaning making, (2) biographical inquiry, (3) the non-conscious, and (4) 'other'.

The approach to the reflections evolved significantly over time. Initially the reflections were very focused on the process and key insights of the interviews. There was no limit to the time dedicated to the reflections, which ended up originally as a long list of notes and insights. After three interviews, it was decided the process was too long; the long list was replaced by mind maps, which were to be created in under 10 minutes. These mind maps identified what was known from the previous interview (reviewed five minutes before) but was also kept open in the current interview. They became a useful tool for building knowledge, testing emerging insights, and mapping how the data was flowing together.

This wave also included a saturation analysis of the interviews–that is, determining the interviews in which the insights started to be repeated with few new insights being added. For example, most of the elements within BI were known by interviews six or seven. In contrast, the definition of meaning making and its true role in the work of coaching continued to develop through all of the interviews.

In the end, the interview-by-interview analysis of Wave 1 would suggest that meaning making was discoverable by BI; that the non-conscious was a vast topic often related to issues in the past, emotions, and other psychology-based practices; and, finally, that reflective practice seemed to have a significant implication on the formation of meaning making.

Wave 2

The second wave of analysis included the coding of the interviews once the full data had been uploaded into NVivo. As noted above, this coding led to 14 nodes.

The node analysis showed that non-conscious, meaning making, and BI were explored in all interviews. The analysis also included the number of references for each node. The number of references indicated just how much the topic was discussed in the interview.

For the non-conscious, the average number of references (i.e., every time that topic was discussed for insight and exploration within the interview) was 4.3. For meaning making, it was 4.9 and for BI it was 9.2. This suggested that, in every interview, there was on average at least four to nine distinct discussions related to the node topic.

The analysis was by no means limited to quantification. For example, there were three interviews in which the non-conscious node appeared only once. However, a review of the transcripts of those three interviews showed that some aspects that could be considered non-conscious were actually coded within BI through the node of 'emotions'. Far from being of little importance to the coach interviewed–as might be inferred from the single mention–it was clear that the non-conscious was in fact a valid area of importance..

The next analysis tool explored in NVivo was flow of conversation. In a majority of the interviews, this analysis showed that the conversation started with an exploration of meaning making, followed equally by either the non-conscious or BI.

Axial Coding and Grouping by Thematic Patterns in the Nodes

The Wave 2 analysis also included axial coding to look for patterns within each node. The non-conscious, meaning making, and BI nodes were the most significant referenced nodes and therefore the first three family themes to emerge. That left 11 nodes to analyze for patterns. Through mind-mapping, the 11 nodes would be grouped into four additional family themes. It should be emphasized that a single node could be an element in more than one family theme. The goal was not to develop mutually exclusive themes, but to develop a list of themes that collectively would include all of the data collected.

The seven themes that emerged from the Wave 2 analysis were the following:

- Theme 1 – Meaning making.
- Theme 2 – Non-conscious.
- Theme 3 – Biographical inquiry.
- Theme 4 – Coach–client relationship.
- Theme 5 – Reflective process.
- Theme 6 – Coaching profession.
- Theme 7 – Psychology.

Here is a quick overview of what we learned about these seven themes from the Wave 2 analysis.

Theme 1 – Meaning making

The interviewees unanimously agreed on meaning making–exploring why clients do what they do–as essential work in coaching. The interviewees were also unanimous in accessing meaning making through BI, although other approaches were mentioned by some. On the other hand, there was no consensus on a clear definition of meaning making or how it is positioned in the field of coaching.

A key takeaway from this analysis was that meaning making appeared to have a multi-dimensionality time dimension–existing in the past, present, and future. Meaning making was also constantly changing and shifting through the coaching conversation and dialogue. This insight has become the starting point of this book and remains one of the key ways to introduce the materiality of why we do biographical work. Meaning making cannot exist without the past, and it is through this inquiry into the past that we can be more aware of what exists in the present and hopefully what might be in the future.

Theme 2 – Non-conscious

All of the interviewees recognized that working with the non-conscious was valuable for any coaching. The largest access point of the non-conscious was bibliographical inquiry (291 references) followed closely by emotions (237 references). Emotions, such as sadness, fear, or shame (as related to escape-based emotions) or happiness, love, or curiosity (as related to attachment-based emotions) were seen as the 'gatekeepers' to what might be happening non-consciously in the client.

The exploration of emotions was often linked to BI via the emotional mechanism associated with memories and experiences in childhood. This insight further compounded the idea of the multidimensional timelines: the past was informing a processing in the present and creating a projection onto the future.

The use of somatic approaches to explore what was really going on, and the awareness of the mind and body connection for both the coach and client, was cited by a number of coaches.

Theme 3 – Biographical inquiry

Under this theme, the major dimensions that were emerging included areas of identity, authority, family of origin, attachment/relationship, and peers/siblings. A context-related dimension included culture, gender roles, and religion. Emotion was also added under this theme despite there being a clear overlap with the non-conscious theme. The reason: much of the work with emotions was related to experiences and/or narratives of the past.

Theme 4 – Coach–client relationship

This theme was a catchall of discussions related to the relationship dynamics between coach and client. Strongly related to the idea of meaning making, this theme was expected to be merged with meaning making in subsequent analysis.

Theme 5 – Reflective process

Every interview gave the interviewee the opportunity to reflect on why, as a coach, they did what they did. This theme reflected the growing recognition of the importance of reflective processing as a key element of dialogical inquiry (the use of discussion to explore meaning).

Theme 6 – Coaching profession

This theme included topics such as ethics, supervision, training, use of assessments, methodology, formulation in coaching, accountability and success factors. While individually not significant, several inferences within this node could be applied to the larger themes of BI, meaning making, and the non-conscious. The exception is the reference, cited by all the interviewees, to 'the nature of coaching'–a phrase that would come to have a significant place in the results of this study.

Theme 7 – Psychology

This final theme was generally classified as psychology but included trauma, healing, psychodynamics, and knowledge areas or theory. All the interview data that contributed to this theme could be weaved into one of the three macro topics of BI, meaning making, or non-conscious.

Wave 3

The third wave of analysis was taking the seven family themes of Wave 2 and adding back the researcher's reflections, the pre-interview data, and what the previous research was saying in relation to these themes, in order to identify the core areas of potential contribution to the knowledge and practice of coaching.

The first step was to code the pre-interview questionnaire responses. The nodes that emerged from this coding were BI, training and knowledge areas, exploration of the conscious and non-conscious, coach–client dynamics and successful outcomes in coaching.

Next, the transcriptions of the pre-interview questionnaires were re-read with these pre-questionnaire nodes in mind. This re-reading led to the creation of a new node called, 'evolving reflections'. This node refers to the evolution of thinking from individual self-reflection (the responses to the questionnaire) to an emergent conversation between two people (the interviews).

The responses in the pre-interview questionnaires and the semi-structured interviews consistently emphasize this idea of reflection as essential to the work of evolving one's thinking. That dialogical inquiry was a source of one's own critical self-reflection became a key finding of this research and will be further explored in Chapter 7.

Eventually, the analysis in Wave 2 suggested significant overlaps in the seven family themes. Working with the insights from the researcher's reflections and pre-interview questionnaire data to create mutually exclusive classifications led to the following three themes:

- Theme 1 – Defining meaning making through dialogical inquiry and BI.
- Theme 2 – A framework for meaning making through BI and an interpretation model.
- Theme 3 – The exploration of the non-conscious as a multi-time, dimension-based intersection of the past, present, and future.

Each of the seven earlier themes and the relevant nodes and insights were incorporated into these three themes.

Wave 4

The fourth and final wave of analysis was based on my reflections as I was writing up the research and the feedback I received when presenting the preliminary findings of the research to my academic advisory group and to audiences in five majors forums: the Science and Art of Coaching Program, the International Coaching Federation (ICF) Community, the Leadership Circle APAC Community, The Singapore Psychological Society, and the 4th Annual Coaches Conclave Conference in India.

During this writing and editorial process, my insights and conclusions from the research continued to evolve. This reflects the iterative nature of emerging insights. In other words, the more times one looks at, reflects on, and identifies key conclusions, the more likely those conclusions will evolve and deeper layers emerge. The finding from this research that through dialogical inquiry (and, by extension, written work), the nature of knowing changes was certainly proven in this Wave 4 of analysis. Each revision of a chapter, and each editing cycle, revealed something deeper or refined something existing.

Much of this process has been captured through multiple phases of analysis, but equally important are the phases of writing and editing, discussed below.

The first phase of the writing revealed the complexity of the research project. There was so much data, continuously overlapping areas of insight, and a lack of clarity on what was relevant material. This phase of writing was first focused on documenting everything possible to ensure that the fullest picture of the data was available. Then editing choices had to be made, and these choices–about what could be said, as well as how these new insights and conclusions could be proven, positioned in the research, and added to the growing body of knowledge–were constantly evolving.

Through the various stages of writing and editing, the confidence and my voice as the practitioner-scholar became stronger, and eventually led to the bold conclusion that this research could possibly expand the nature of coaching. Reaching this conclusion was an iterative process. The more time spent on the research, and the more time the literature was explored, the more it became clear that expanding the nature of coaching was the scaffolding that held the other insights. How can models be created for areas that have not been linked to the nature of the work being done in coaching? The practice was growing faster than the profession could match, and therefore it was considered essential to contribute to the definitions and nature of coaching as much as it was to present new frameworks for exploration with clients.

Materiality of Findings

Eventually, as a result of Wave 4, the major themes evolved slightly to become the following:

- Expanding the nature of coaching within a third-generation perspective.
- The use of BI in coaching.
- Using the intersection of the past, present, and future to explore the non-conscious in coaching.

The third theme is the one with the most material insights to this whole study. Because it set the stage for the rest of the book, this theme– using the intersection of the past, present, and future to explore the non-conscious in coaching– was described in Chapter 1. The remaining two themes will be explored in more detail in the following chapters. Chapter 4 discusses the concept of the 'third generation' of coaching, which expands the nature of coaching. Chapters 5, 6, and 7 will cover the use of BI in coaching. Chapter 5 focuses on the rationale for BI in coaching, and discusses expanding the nature of coaching; Chapter 6 describes the six dimensions of the Biographical Dimensions of Meaning Making framework; and Chapter 7 closes out this section on BI with a discussion on what BI tells us.

CHAPTER 4

Expanding the Nature of Coaching: A Third-Generation Perspective

As described in Chapter 3, one of the three key findings that emerged from this research is that incorporating meaning making, biographical inquiry (BI), and the non-conscious into coaching was shifting the nature of the work done in coaching. This research thus requires expanding the nature of coaching. This expansion fits best in the concept of a third generation of coaching, a concept with roots in the recent explosive growth of coaching. This chapter will explore how I am proposing to expand the definition of coaching within this third-generation format, and may even begin to give way to the next generation of coaching–a generation that is beginning to take root and will hopefully flourish through further empirical research into these vast topics.

Rapid Growth and New Ideas

The coaching profession has expanded at an astronomical rate in this millennia, with the majority of this growth happening in the past decade. In 2006, the coaching profession counted approximately 30,000 certified professional coaches globally, with industry revenues totalling US$1.5 billion (ICF, 2006). By 2016, the number of coaches totalled more than 53,000 certified professional coaches, with more coaches joining the profession every year, and annual revenues

Expanding the Nature of Coaching

had almost doubled to just under U$3 billion (ICF, 2016). As of 2022, PWC estimates the coaching industry size at US$4.5B; it is considered the second fastest-growing global sector with more than 109,000 coaches worldwide.

The unprecedented growth of the industry led inexorably to an explosion of coaching philosophies–some of them rooted in psychology given the large number of new coaches moving over from the field of psychology. Psychological knowledge and practice are integral parts of coaching as they consider the behaviour and emotion of the client and how these relate to learning and change (Passmore and Fillery-Travis, 2011). The result was the emergence of the discipline of coaching psychology, which leveraged the use of applied psychology to the practice of coaching. However, there is a lagging pace to the research due to the lack of collaboration between practitioners and academics, unlike in other professions such as psychology, medicine, chemistry, and law (Fillery-Travis and Corrie (2019). As explained in Chapters 2 and 3, the research study at the heart of this book builds on coaching research but is firmly positioned in coaching psychology, with additional contributions from the disciplines of applied neuroscience and psychology.

Divergent Views on the Nature of Coaching

As coaching has evolved, the injection of new ideas and techniques has led to confusion about its precise nature and what it is designed to achieve (Ives, 2008). Compounding the confusion is that the research in the field of coaching and coaching psychology has not merged with the speed and pace of the practice (Fillery-Travis and Corrie, 2019). The arrival of new ideas and techniques has led to multiple, divergent views on the precise nature of coaching, including both the purpose of coaching, and the process through which that purpose can be achieved. One perspective argues that the purpose of coaching is to change behaviour by helping a client set and achieve goals. An opposing view is that the purpose of coaching is to offer a meaning-making process to the client; meaning making may result in behaviour change, or it may not (Cunningham, 2017).

A number of researchers exploring these questions about the nature of coaching offer different frameworks or prisms through which to view 21st century coaching. The most relevant of these approaches in the context of the research of this book is the concept of a third generation of coaching, which was proposed–separately–by two researchers, Reinhard Stelter of the University of

Copenhagen and Anthony Grant of the University of Sydney. Before exploring this third generation of coaching, it may be helpful to understand how coaching has evolved over time. First-generation coaching was a goal-centric model, designed to help a client achieve some type of behavioural change. As coaching grew, so did the nature of the work done in coaching. As such, second-generation coaching believed more strongly in the innate capacity and wisdom within the client and assumes the client has the solution within themselves. But again, over time, third-generation coaching moved into a more profound focus on values and identity work (Stelter, 2014).

It is important to note that Grant and Stelter define third-generation coaching differently. For Stelter, third-generation coaching places a stronger emphasis on *values* and *meaning-making work* than traditional coaching. The role of a coach is to explore, through reflection and a narrative process, the identity of the client (Stelter, 2014). For Grant, on the other hand, third-generation coaches use high-quality conversations to improve the *performance* and *well-being* of their clients.

Despite these differences, third-generation coaching for both researchers is based on coaching psychology and involves deeper identity-related work through high-quality meaningful conversations and reflections–and there is now a growing empirical base of research to support these claims. However, as discussed in Chapter 2, there is still a large deficit in the research exploring how meaning making links with biographical data, for which empirical proof is provided through the research in this book.

In this chapter, we describe how the findings in this research correlates with the expanded view of coaching proposed by Stelter and Grant's descriptions of third-generation coaching. Specifically, we will explore two key themes that emerged from the data:

- Expanding the view of coaching as a collaborative process of dialogical inquiry and reflective practice.
- Expanding the access points of meaning making in coaching.

Expanding the View of Coaching as a Collaborative Process

Coaching as a collaborative process between coach and client was a constant theme in the interviews. For a majority of the interviewees, the role of a coach was to *generate insights* or to act as a *catalyst* for ideas and understanding. Most interviewees also saw an explicit attempt to *accelerate change* in the client as another goal of coaching. Finally, more than half noted the *reflective partnership* the coach needed to establish with clients. However they described it, all of the interviewees agreed: the collaborative process was an essential part of coaching.

The Academic Research on Coaching Collaboration

While this perspective of coach as collaborator is not new, it has not been significantly well researched. For example, Grant (2016) emphasized that coaches should focus on the well-being of their clients through higher-quality conversations, but he provides no model or framework for these higher-quality conversations. Stelter (2014) proposed four dimensions of a narrative-based collaborative approach to coaching–coaching as a reflective space, coaching and meaning making, coaching as a post-modern space of learning and development, and coaching in promoting dialogical and reflective leadership–but likewise provides no frameworks for a reflective space process or the actual process of identifying meaning making.

Other studies focus on the impact of the coach-client relationship on the collaborative coaching process but, again, fail to offer any frameworks for structuring and enhancing the relationship to improve coaching outcomes.

The research on the reflective process in coaching is divided among three areas of study: the reflective process for the client; the reflective process of the coach; and how knowledge and power might impact the collaboration between coach and client (Hébert, 2015). Extensive research is available for the first two areas of study, but not the third. Yet, it is through the dynamic of knowledge and power that reflection can play an important role in anchoring the dialogical process. One avenue of research into this dynamic is to analyze the complexity of coaching as a series of reflective practices coming together. Another potential avenue of research is to develop a process or framework to explore the historical circumstances that might shape a coach's subjective experience and knowledge (Cushion, 2015). After all, before coaches can engage in reflection, they must understand the impact of these historical circumstances.

As we leave the existing research behind, let's explore how the research in this book addresses the two pillars of coaching as a collaborative process: (1) reflective meta-practice and (2) dialogical inquiry.

Reflective Meta-Practice: The Coach Begins with the Self

All of the interviewees used some form of reflective practice in coaching, whether for self-reflection (to reflect about themselves), or within the coaching work itself. As part of the reflective practice in coaching, a coach might seek to elicit insights from the client through intellectual, emotional, and/or somatic-driven responses, as exemplified in these interview excerpts:

- 'I find myself moving between a cognitive exploration to an intuition-based one.' (Intellectual response)
- 'It's when I get emotional that magic really begins.' (Emotion-driven response)
- 'When I feel my body reacting to the discussion, I use it as data for us both to explore deeper.' (Somatic response)

These responses are not simply reactions to the client. It can take years of reflective practice for a coach to successfully find the pathway (i.e., 'access') to the client, as the following quote illustrates:

"I have always self-identified as an intuitive coach, but that left me wanting in terms of coherent practice. Through years of reflective practice, I see how my own journeying

through different psychotherapeutic models as both patient and clinician, my own dysfunctional early life experiences from family of origin, my work as a consultant and coach and trainer–it all contributed to the messy palette of colour that informs my intuition. I used to hold that outside of my work with client[s], but now I bring it into the room, into the conversation as part of my coherent practice".

Dialogical Inquiry: Co-creating the Helping Environment

The other facet of a coaching collaboration is the conversation itself, including the flow between the coach and client and the engagement of both in the conversation–all of which make up what is called in this book the 'dialogical process'. A little more than half of the interviewees referred to the importance of the conversation to coaching. One interviewee noted that there was no template for such a conversation, as the content of any conversation is based on where both the coach and the client are in their respective journeys at the time.

Analysis of the interviews revealed five core areas of exploration that influenced the dialogical inquiry process, beginning with, as mentioned above, what was happening with the client, and what was happening with the coach, but also including the intent or the goals of the coaching; the coaching relationship; and the coaching system.

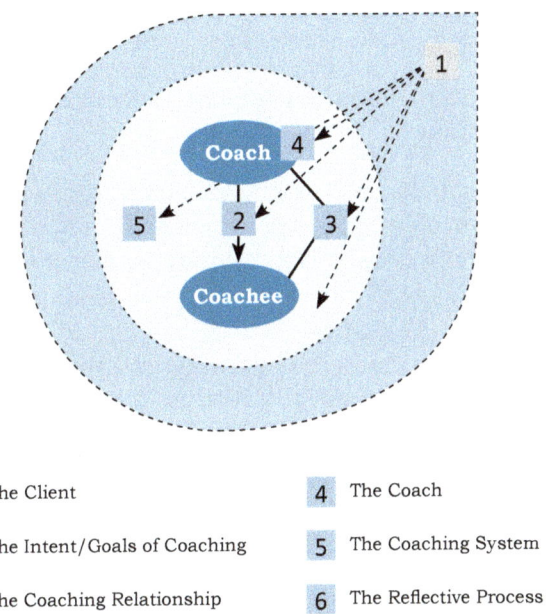

1. The Client
2. The Intent/Goals of Coaching
3. The Coaching Relationship
4. The Coach
5. The Coaching System
6. The Reflective Process

Figure 4.1 - Six Nodes of Higher Quality Conversations in Coaching (6-HQC)

These five core areas of exploration along with the dialogical inquiry itself comprise the elements or 'nodes' of my dialogical inquiry model, called 'The Six Nodes of Higher-Quality Conversations in Coaching' (6-HQC), which is illustrated in Figure 4.1 below. This model describes, as follows, how the six core nodes of the coaching conversation interact to make meaning:

1– The Dialogical Inquiry & Reflective Process

This first node is the most critical aspect of this overall model. It is to this node that all other nodes will come back to, in order to expand the thinking, shift perspectives, and gain insights. Interviewees spoke to this critical part of the collaborative process of coaching, which is called reflective processing. It is this first node that is the explicitly designated space for conversation and reflection about what is really going on, incorporating the collaborative meaning with the Client (node 2) and the Coach (node 3). In this space occurs what interviewees variously referred to as *'catching the flow', 'being a participant', 'acting as catalyst', 'hearing potential', 'sensing before client', 'obligation to name', 'really seeing',* and *'reflective partner.'* In most coaching models, this area for insight is either exclusively held within the coach, or inferred as part of the process. In this model, the reflective process is being held as an essential part of the dialogical process and the most essential space to make meaning.

In node 1, the coach's reflection will reveal what is happening within themselves, as exemplified by these statements that describe the impact of dialogical inquiry on the coach: *'I find myself moving between a cognitive exploration to an intuition-based one'*, *'I use my fear and bravery, I am connected and vulnerable'*, *'When I see my own story coming out,'* *'It's when I get emotional that magic really begins'*, and *'When I feel my body reacting to the discussion.'* Within this node will be where there is space for the client to also come back, to reflect, to find new meaning, and to use all the same elements at the disposal of the coach to do their integration work.

2 – The Client

This second node of consideration is the meaning-making system of the client, through which they extract meaning from the past, make meaning in the present, and project meaning into the future. Exploring the meaning-making system of the client is foundational to all coaching. While the client exists as its own entity (e.g., within this second node), it is the movement between node 1 (the designated space of dialogical inquiry and reflective process) to node 2 that brings the essential meaning making held in this node into focus. In the movement from node 2 to node 1, and then back to node 2, is where the client can assess their agency over the topics revealed in the meaning making, creating the opportunity for real integration and shifts.

3 – The Intent/Goals of the Coaching

Node 3 contains the core objectives and goals of the work. It is essential to include the contracting of going into the past as an explicit goal. A coach can expand on the original intent of the coaching without losing its core goal. It is in node 3 that the coach draws out any risk of trauma from past history, and considers whether therapy and/or counselling, which would sit outside the coaching, is called for. Finally, the coach would share any formulation related to the client's goals–a formulation that explains the need to go into the past. This node is revisited several times throughout the course of the coaching engagement.

4 – The Coaching Relationship

The coaching relationship is absolutely vital to the success of this coaching model. Eight-five percent of interviewees felt developing a

Expanding the Nature of Coaching

partnership with clients to be an important aspect to the work of coaching. The relationship can vary; interviewees were divided on the most important function of the coach in the partnership, with some emphasizing the coach as a catalyst (62 percent), a reflective partner (54 percent), or as an accelerator for change (70 percent). By holding the relationship within node 1, both coach and client can explore what is happening in the relationship, what works and what does not, and how the role each person in the relationship is developing. The insights that emerged from node 1 are then reintegrated into node 4, allowing the relationship dynamic to keep evolving.

5 - The Coach

This node captures the coach's intuition and reading of emotional data, which allows them to see into the non-conscious patterns that may be emerging–not only in relation to the client but for the coach as well. When the intelligence and/or interpretation resulting from the coach's intuition is moved to the reflection space of node 1, the coach will see their own patterns or insights.

6 – The Coaching System

In the research at the heart of this book, we do not focus on the system that exists around the client and coach but rather on the interaction and meaning making between coach and client. That is not to say that the system is not important. In fact, much of the current research over the past 15 years has been almost exclusively focused on systemic coaching approaches. The system includes, for example, the sponsors of the coaching; the primary stakeholders and how their needs impact the work done in coaching; and the culture of the organization and inferred privileges or judgments that exist around those who get coaching. This is an essential place of consideration. Taking these elements into node 1 for reflection and expansion, and then back can lead to important insights for the client.

All of these elements are woven together and influence each other in the dialogical inquiry process, which, as one interviewee put it, *'can make your head spin'*. Another interviewee characterized dialogical inquiry as *'a cycle where you get alongside people and support them to go where they wish to go. So, we co-create the helping environment to work with them'*. The challenge, according to this interviewee, is that co-creating this helping environment requires, on the part of the coach, *'reaching out to test oneself, to inquire into and within, to test the environment, test the client, test the relationship and to bring that back to the self again, I mean, it's an ongoing loop.'* The bottom line here being that nothing exists on its own. In coaching, we are required to bring all these nodes into a dialogical and reflective place (node 1) to reflect what is happening in the coaching process and how new meaning is being constantly created.

Expanding the Access Points of Meaning Making in Coaching

'Access points' of meaning-making refers to the pathways or doors that a coach can use to help a client's meaning-making efforts–pathways or doors that need to be 'opened' by both the coach and the client. As one interviewee explained it:

"In coaching, we actually need to share a common starting point so that our frames of reference are clear. This research is an opportunity for the beginnings of a worldwide understanding of what the starting point could be as it relates to meaning making".

The search for access points of meaning making benefit from the inclusion of psychological knowledge in the field of coaching psychology.

Exploring the behaviour, thinking processes, and emotions of the client depend in great part on psychology (Passmore and Fillery-Travis, 2011).

Which leads us to review the question of what exactly is meaning making and how can it be explored in coaching.

Earlier in this book, we described the use of narration to explore meaning making. The narrative process helps clients become aware of the stories that shape their conception of reality. We also described the meaning-making approach based on constructive-developmental psychology, which helps clients explore the interaction of the self with their environments and how that journey can expand and contract based on their own cognitive, emotional, and well-being factors.

These two approaches are going in different directions: narrative practice considers lifespan experiences but lacks a comprehensive framework to guide the exploration, while constructive-developmental psychology moves away from traditional lifespan exploration into staged growth but loses the insights lifespan work can provide. Current research has missed entirely the intersection of meaning making with a guided and framed examination of lifespan experiences–or, as we are calling it, BI.

The Expansion of Meaning Making in Coaching

The data from this book's research is clear: meaning making is essential to the work of coaching. The interviewees were unanimous in this position. In addition, for a significant majority of the interviewees, meaning making was ultimately the main purpose of coaching. As one interviewee explained: *'Meaning making is essentially how clients are making sense of the worlds they're in or the dilemmas they're facing, which is ultimately the work of coaching'*. Another interviewee declared:

> *"We need to stop looking at meaning making as a theoretical framework in the sense of Freud's theoretical framework or Jung, or Gestalt or anybody else. It's what we do in coaching the whole time, which is make meaning in everything we do, think, and feel in life".*

Third-generation coaching sees coaching as a meaning-making process. With such strong evidence in the data that coaching is the work of meaning making, the implications for the nature of coaching are twofold:

1. The definition of coaching and the bodies of research related to coaching should be more focused on meaning making.

2. If meaning making is a sense-making exercise of all the events in one's life, a more deliberate exploration of the client's life events should be considered as part of coaching.

Can coaching uncover the source of meaning making in a way that is different from the existing paradigms of narration or constructive-developmental approaches? One interviewee's metaphor describes how a more deliberate exploration of lifespan differs from narrative practice:

"We need to look at it a bit like doing core ice samples. Within the core sample, you can see the history of the earth. This is a bit like storytelling, through the little stories we hold about our lives, you get information from different layers of a core, but you need to test those layers through some form of deliberate lifespan exploration".

Accessing Meaning Making from our Biographical Histories

In the previous section, we reviewed how meaning making needs to be positioned as the core purpose of coaching. This section drills down to explore how the access points of meaning making can be expanded.

In coaching psychology, meaning making is accessed through narration. However, current coaching psychology approaches don't help coaches understand which areas of a person's life story should be explored. The narrative process focuses on dimensions such as personal event memory, the organization of specific memories across their lifespan and momentous events. However, the intent of the process is to examine the evolution of the stories and how they reflect the client's progress, rather than what the content of the stories reveals about the client.

Likewise, constructive-developmental approaches focus on the maturity of the ego–i.e., the maturity of individuals at stages in their lives–rather than, again, focusing on what the content of the stories reveal. Because the life events *per se* are not the point of inquiry, little to no consideration is given to explicitly exploring them.

This lack of attention to the content of stories from a research point of view needs to be addressed since the data shows that many coaches have incorporated BI into their practices. All of the interviewees referred to explicitly exploring life events in the client's biographical history to access meaning making. In total, the interviewees made 242 distinct references to biographical exploration with clients.

One interviewee captures through the metaphor of a painting the importance of a client's biography to meaning making:

"I think part of the BI process is that it allows the person to stand in front of themselves, much like viewing a painting at a gallery, and begin to acquire levels of understanding that previously they haven't visited or contemplated that way before and haven't had a framework within which to think about themselves. And then I think that establishes a sense of meaning making of themselves in their life. That becomes hugely significant for them and very rewarding".

In conclusion, I am now offering a new definition of coaching that resides within this third-generation view. My offering is to define coaching as a *meaning-making* process that explores the *past, present, and future* to facilitate *developmental shifts.* To examine each aspect of this definition we explore these three facets:

1. Meaning making: The process of the client (with mutual support from the coach) to understand, make sense of, and then respond to things that happen.
2. Time dimension: How our response mechanism (conscious and non-conscious)

stem from the experiences we have had/aspire to have over a lifetime.
3. Developmental shifts: Where the goals of coaching can continually shift and move as deeper exploration is uncovered in coaching in order to serve the client

CHAPTER 5

The Rationale for Biographical Inquiry

As described in Chapter 3, the analysis of the research study led to three core findings.

1. Expanding the nature of coaching within a third-generation perspective.
2. Using biographical inquiry (BI) in coaching.
3. Using the intersection of the past, present, and future to explore the non-conscious in coaching.

I began this book with the last insight: the intersection of the past, present, and future. In Chapter 3, we explored expanding the nature of coaching in a third-generation perspective and I offered a new definition of coaching within this context. In Chapters 5 and 6, I will focus on the second core finding of using BI in coaching and the framework that covers a comprehensive inquiry with clients. This chapter focuses on the rationale for doing BI work with clients and the key outcomes that result from this type of inquiry.

Four Reasons to Use Biographical Inquiry in Coaching

In order to develop a comprehensive model for BI, it is important to understand clearly the rationale for using BI in coaching. The data from the research showed that all the interviewees used

BI as part of their coaching process. In addition to exploring meaning making through the client's biography, as discussed in the previous chapter, the research identified four specific reasons why BI was an essential process in coaching:

1. To create a shared understanding of the client that acknowledges diversity.
2. To shift aspects of the non-conscious into consciousness.
3. To apply a formulation approach to coaching.
4. To create trust in coaching.

Rationale 1: To Create a Shared Understanding that Acknowledges Diversity

'When I am exploring with clients,' explained one interviewee, *'I often say, I want to explore what happened to you in the process of growing up, so to the best of my ability, I can share those experiences with you and learn to see the world as you do'.* Creating a shared understanding of their clients through knowing their life stories, and through that knowledge better understanding how they view the world, is one of the most important reasons for exploring the life and background of a client.

Creating a shared understanding between coach and client is essential for coaches to identify and make sense of the issues that clients are dealing with, why those issues have arisen–notably, how the roots of those issues may be found in past events–and, eventually, what solutions coaches can prescribe to clients to deal with those issues. This 'formulation' approach, and the role of BI in implementing it, will be explored in detail later in this chapter.

Of particular relevance to the research in this book is the importance of using BI to create a shared understanding that acknowledges and appreciates the influence of diversity on meaning making. Appreciating the biographical data that related to diversity, equity, and inclusion was particularly relevant to interviewees in this study because of the multi-cultural context in which most of them were working as coaches. More than three-quarters of the interviewees were living and/or working in a country–and for many in a region of the world–that was not their place of birth. And all of the interviewees were working with a very diverse group of clients of different cultures, religions, race, gender self-identity, and age.

The process of creating a shared understanding of the client was made more complex because the interviewees were often supporting clients

The Rationale for Biographical Inquiry

through their own cross-cultural experience; that is, the clients they were working with looked, acted, and behaved differently from themselves. Not surprisingly, the topic of diversity and cross-cultural considerations was raised in nearly all of the interviews, with specific references made to culture, spirituality, and race and/or ethnicity. Raising these topics was part of the coaches' efforts to better understand the client and to explore with the client the context drivers that might be influencing or driving their behaviour.

To illustrate the challenge of working with different cultural backgrounds, note that Asia, where this study took place, consists of 48 countries with 6 sub-regions, each with their own unique culture. The Southeast Asian culture is very different from the culture in Central Asia, to take just two examples. Even within the sub-regions, there are significant cultural differences. In Southeast Asia, for example, people in the Philippines will express themselves very differently from people in Singapore.

One can see the importance for the coach, in any effort to create a shared understanding of the client, to explore the client's unique cultural dynamics and surface how those cultural dynamics might impact or influence the beliefs, attitudes, and behaviour of the client.

Acquiring a good understanding of a new

culture, with some elements that might be more nuanced and less visible than others, has always been a challenge, but even more so today. The reason is that in today's digital age, the traditional cultural divides of geography and language can be much more easily breached than in the past. For that reason, one must be careful not to make assumptions about a given culture. One interviewee eloquently described the challenge of the digital era's 'diffusion culture':

"Influences are now extending beyond the family and our geographic location because of the impact of digitization on young people. This whole idea of culture becomes almost obsolete because there's an osmosis and a fluidity in the level of the way influences are coming in and from many directions. For example, that child who sits here in Singapore is watching American TV and watching how a family behaves there. So, we see them emulating cultures they have never experienced first-hand. I am calling this a diffusion culture because knowing where someone grew up is not enough to know what cultures they most identify with".

Even when a coach and client might share the same cultural backgrounds, the interviewees suggested that sameness cannot be assumed because it is impossible to know all of the influences on a client. There will no doubt be influences that are unknown and yet likely to be different. Thus, a coach must put the work in to creating a shared understanding of what drives their clients without relying on any assumptions or pre-conceived notions. And because these drivers may exist on a conscious or a non-conscious level, a shared understanding is best explored through BI.

Past research is more likely to focus on approaches to be used to reach a shared understanding between coach and client. For example, the formulation approach mentioned at the beginning of this section was proposed by Lane and Corrie (2009) as a framework to capture and present the shared understanding results of the coach-client BI collaboration.

In general, the influence of diversity, equity and inclusion (DEI) factors in developing a shared understanding is under-explored in the coaching research. One reason may be that most research tends to be driven by Western cultures, where the depth of diversity in society is different as in the Asian cultures that formed the background of my research. As a result, the research from these Western cultures holds a potentially different perspective and underpinning that is skewed based on the needs that drive those societies. Controlling for bias and prejudice becomes more difficult, particularly in today's society due to globalization and increasing diversity within communities where these empirical research studies are being conducted. With that being said, there is research that offers some quality data related to this topic. Pillemer (1998) showed that autobiographical considerations help uncover the cultural and gender assumptions a client has formed over a lifetime. More recently, Passmore (2010) suggests that effective coaching requires the consideration of the diversity of the client as a theme. For example, he cautioned that coaches who don't examine their own cultural heritage first might let their subtle ethnocentric biases lead them to misinterpret a client's motivations and other personal attributes–a potentially serious misstep in the application of BI. Additionally, as explored by Rankin-Wright et all (2017), themes around negotiating identities, privilege, and blind spots as well the presence of systemic discrimination are often cited as issues that emerge in coaching–although past research offers little to no support on how to solve these challenges.

Rationale 2: To Shift the Non-conscious into Consciousness

'Many people, particularly very senior leaders, haven't spent a lot of time in their lives, reflecting upon who they are, and why they have become the person that they are. By exploring BI, the consequence is kind of outlining the beginnings, or to lift into consciousness, a person's awareness of themselves in a way that is often both a delight and a surprise to themselves'.

Expert from Interview

To somehow dive into the darkness of the non-conscious and bring it into the light of the conscious is not an easy task–and yet, through BI, it seems to be something that often happens as a type of consequence to that kind of inquiry. More than half of the interviewees said moving things out from the non-conscious into consciousness was an important function–and strength–of BI work. The client of one interviewee felt this type of exploration through BI was more effective than 20 years of therapy. The reason, according to the client, was that the coach was helping them discover how their life stories had shaped their current perspectives; the therapist was focused on healing the trauma.

One interviewee offered a succinct explanation of how, through BI, a client can be made to see what was previously unseen:

"Often, I may ask a question or share a perspective, and then the person would say 'I'd never thought of it like that before'. And you can actually sense that they've acquired a different layer of meaning about themselves in that instant moment".

What was evident through the research was that all the interviewees who used BI were doing so because of an explicit choice they knew was not traditionally part of the world of coaching. Either they were trained in psychology or they had, over years of experience as a coach, discovered that the past is always in the room and therefore deserves and needs space for exploration. Being able to interact with those life stories somehow changed their meaning in the present, and yet, there is so little in coaching research that speaks to this phenomenon.

Past coaching research into shifting the non-conscious into consciousness through exploration of a client's biography is sparse. Instead, a review of past research in coaching reveals a clear bias in favour of a future orientation while the past is ignored. Rothaizer and Hill (2009) criticize this future-orientation bias, which they attribute to an emphasis in coaching on the 'what now' instead of the 'why'. With understanding the 'why' pushed to the background, the motivation to explore the past is equally shunted aside.

Rothaizer and Hill are in the minority. Multiple studies support the future-orientated view in coaching, arguing, for example, that this approach helps individuals cope with stress and protects people from depression (Zheng et al., 2019) or that it is positively associated with work effort, proactive career behaviours, and career adaptability (Praskova and Johnson, 2021).

Despite the issue of past vs future orientation, the non-conscious is gaining greater attention in coaching notably from the perspective of inner self-identity work. Dodwell (2020) introduced the idea of recovering through coaching a client's 'lost sense of self'. In other words, clients may only have a partial picture of self because much of it is hidden in the non-conscious.

As for the coaching psychology field, it borrows from psychoanalytic theory a psychodynamic approach to coaching, which depends in great part on exploration of the unconscious, such as unconscious anxieties and defences. However, the research is mostly silent on how this psychodynamic approach links to BI and the non-conscious.

Rationale 3: To Apply a Formulation Approach to Coaching

"In England, if you set out to buy a house, you're well advised to have what's called 'a structural survey'. Experts come in and have a serious look at what the condition of the house is from the point of view of the way the whole thing is working. Find what the possible problems could be. I think a BI is quite an interesting way of conducting a structural survey of the person in order that you both [coach and client] have got some sense of who this person has become over the course of their life."

Expert from Interview

A key element of the methodology used for the research in this book was the ongoing reflections and adjustments made between each interview– thus every interview impacted the design of the interviews that followed. The importance of this iterative process is evident in this section of the chapter, which argues that another major reason for using BI is to develop a *formulation* for the client. An approach borrowed directly from psychology, a formulation is the outcome of a coach working with a client to *capture and summarize in words the issues of a client*, *explanations for the existence of these issues, and potential solutions.*

The idea of formulation as a contribution of BI did not appear until the seventh interview, although previous interviews had laid the groundwork for this notion. In the very first interview, excerpted above, the interviewee introduced the idea of BI as a sort of 'structural test'–a complete overview of who the client is or has become as a person and potential issues that might lie ahead. As the interviews progressed, the notion of BI *predicting* future issues began to solidify. More than half of the interviewees felt that biographical data could provide a model for how the client might likely behave under certain circumstances, which could then give coaches more conscious choices of how to shift the client's behaviour.

The idea of formulation introduced in the seventh interview, however, is much more appropriate and salient to this research as it emphasizes *exploration into the past* as the source of any hypotheses for the future. This interviewee explains the contribution of BI-driven formulation to coaching:

"I look at biographical data as a process of formulation, which comes from applied psychology. Through this approach, I can really see someone. And equally, they

feel seen right through, which can be very confronting. But this developing of hypotheses about what might be going on for them through an examination of their life and family relationships can be quite informative and useful".

In terms of prior research, Lane and Corrie (2009), as mentioned above, proposed the application of formulation in coaching. Of particular value was their definition of formulation as 'an explanatory account of the issues with which a client is presenting (including predisposing, precipitating, and maintaining factors) that can form the basis of a shared framework of understanding, and which has implications for change'.

Formulation in coaching was further explored by Kovacs and Corrie (2021), who argued that based on a formulation approach, a coach can design and implement an intervention relevant to the client. Building on Kovacs and Corrie's perspectives on shared understanding, BI can be used as a formulation approach for three reasons: it helps a coach create a descriptive understanding of the client; it evolves with additional understanding and insights; and it has some predictive power.

Rationale 4: Source of Trust Creation within Coaching

One important benefit to BI is the trust that is developed through the exploration. Nearly every interviewee stated that trust, attachment, and/or the relationship between the coach and client was significantly improved through the sharing of biographical data. There was only one interviewee who had a contrary view, insisting that all trust in coaching was based on competence alone.

Trust is both an outcome and a driver of BI. The sharing of the client's biography creates the trust of the client in the coach, which in turns allows the coach to, as one interviewee explained, 'raise more challenging issues because [clients] feel safe, they are more likely to share with you some of the things that they may not share otherwise.' Without this mutual trust between client and coach, the deep dive into the client's non-conscious and conscious history is significantly hampered. As the previously quoted interviewee explains, trust *'gets you below the surface, away from transactional conversations, to talking about meaning and how they make sense of the world and what might be driving that so you can learn more easily.'*

Clients feel through BI that the coach is making a sincere attempt to understand them, and the resulting trust in the coach is for many clients a key factor in the success of the coaching, as described by this interviewee speaking of a past client:

"I have a really great client that I've worked with for a few years, but I don't talk to her very often now because she's high flying and she's doing super well. She has had many coaches but sees our work together as the most successful. One of the reasons why she thinks our coaching was effective is that I spent our first session focused on getting to know her and her history. To really see her created trust in her and our partnership. She claims that trust with me is why we were set on the path for success".

The academic research in coaching is in agreement that positive coaching outcomes can only occur once trust in the coach-client relationship is established. 'Cultivates Trust and Safety' is in fact one of the core competencies listed by the International Coaching Federation (2019).

There is, however, less of a consensus among researchers on how one establishes trust. One study identified ability, benevolence, and integrity as the three essential factors for successful coaching with, in the view of more experienced coaches, benevolence being the most critical factor in establishing trust. Benevolent coaches are well meaning and kind, and convey to the client that they want to be of service–they want to help in any way they can. Trying to really understand and get to know the client was a clear manifestation in the eyes of clients of this benevolence (Shiemann et al., 2019). While benevolence is not the only way to establish trust, it is a key factor, and explains why BI is an effective approach.

In conclusion, the four elements described in this chapter–shared understanding, shifting consciousness, a formulation approach, and trust creation–provide a powerful justification for coaching that is built on BI. Figure 5.1 shows a framework uniting these four key drivers of the use of BI.

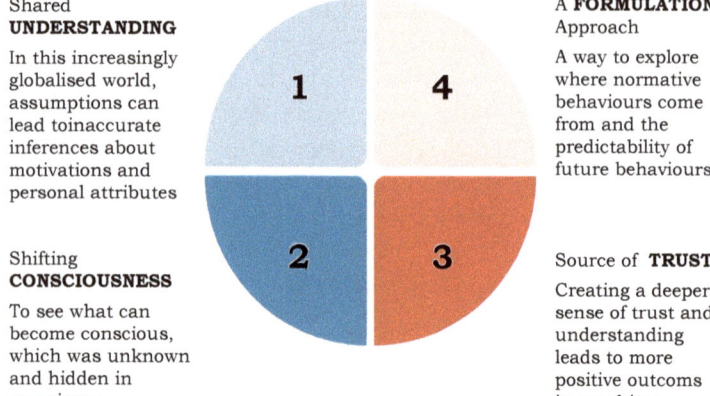

Figure 5.1 The four drivers for conducting biographical inquiry in coaching

CHAPTER 6

The Six Dimensions of Biographical Inquiry

In this chapter, we review the six dimensions of biographical inquiry (BI) that emerged from the research. After coding and analysis, a dozen topics related to BI were identified in the interviews. All of the interviewees explored their clients' *family of origin* (parents, siblings, extended family), *identity*, *authority structures* (including parents, teachers, and bosses), *emotions* (emotional expression, emotional dynamism), and *relationship/attachment dynamics*. A majority also explored *culture, religion, race, spirituality, and cross-cultural influencing factors*; *socioeconomic factors*; and *sibling/peer dynamics*. About half explored *traumas* (including health issues) and *generational drivers*. A small number of interviewees discussed topics categorized as *other* (such as birthing story, ancestry exploration) and *affiliated culture* (social media impact). These 12 topics explored by the interviewees were revised based on overlaps (e.g., family of origin research included siblings but was also a standalone area of inquiry). In addition, anything explored by only one or two interviewees was excluded from this list. In the end, there were six remaining topic areas: *hierarchy, peers, identity, context, emotional spectrum*, and *relationship*.

These six topics were analyzed in the context of the existing academic research (herein referred to as secondary research) in three disciplines:

Psychology. In psychology, the most relevant content in BI was family of origin research, which encompassed many dimensions including parents, siblings, attachment dynamics, normative behaviour, identity, and emotional processing (Hovestadt et al., 1985; Leifman, 2001; Hemming et al., 2012).

Coaching. As described in chapter 2, BI was applied in coaching through the HASIE model (Brown and Brown, 2012), which is adapted from the applied neurosciences. The HASIE model explores hierarchy, attachment dynamics, peer-based dynamics, identity, and emotional tapestry.

Coaching psychology. In coaching psychology, the BI approach used most often is from a narrative perspective, in which meaning making is gleaned from the client's stories of life events.

Looking at the family of origin research in psychology, the HASIE research, and narrative practice research, combined with the central themes covered in the interviews, the following six areas represent a comprehensive list of the core dimensions required for exploration in BI. These six topic areas became the six dimensions of the Biographical Dimensions of Meaning Making framework, as shown in Figure 6.1.

Biographical Dimensions of Meaning Making© (BDMM)

Emotional Spectrum

An exploration of the emotional capacity of the client over the full spectrum of escape to attachment emotions.

Hierarchy

An exploration of the evolving authority structure(s) in the client's life.

Peers

An exploration of peer-based dynamics including siblings, friends and the chosen family.

Context

An exploration of the socioeconomic, cultural and environmental influences on the client's life over time.

Identity

An exploration of the evolving sense of self from inherited to constructed identity.

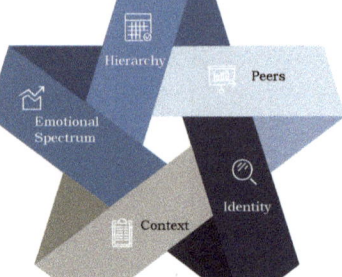

Relationship

Encompassing the whole structure is the capacity to form and sustain relationships.

Figure 6.1. Biographical Dimensions of Meaning Making

In this chapter, we will explore each of these six dimensions of BDMM© more fully.

Hierarchy

The terms from the interviews that were placed in this first dimension were: *family of origin* (including family, families); *extended family* (including uncles, aunts); *parents* (including parent, parented, parenting, grandparents, primary caregivers); *authority*; *boss* (including bosses); *previous generation* (including ancestors); and *teacher*.

In all the interviews, the interviewees evoked some form of exploration with their clients around the role of Hierarchy (as outlined by these terms). With its 180 mentions, 'family of origin', which referred to the core family unit of the interviewee, was the most common place of inquiry.

Within Hierarchy, six core themes were explored:
- The traits of the clients' parents/primary caregivers including occupation, personality, and engagement with household.
- Power structure dynamics within the clients' family including reward and punishment.
- 'Isms' of the family that created the normative views on behaviours within the household.

- 'Echoes' from previous generations informing the way the family interacted.
- Reinforcing experiences with other authority structures.
- Authority expression in organizational life.

Traits of Parents Including Occupation, Personality and Engagement with Household

All the interviewees explored parental*[1] dynamics with their clients in one form or another. Often seen as the easiest entrance point to learn more about the context of family life for the client, the request to 'Tell me more about your parents' was often used. Sixty-two percent of the interviewees used some form of this phrase to begin their exploration via BI.

Past secondary research has linked adult leadership traits to parental traits, for example when idealized leadership images mirror descriptions of one's parental traits (Keller, 1999). Other research shows that a parents' traits can become the idealized traits of a leader, assuming of course the parents were respected and admired by the client (Magomaeva, 2013). Parents may also become the model of leadership

---

[1] * references to parents here always include 'primary caregivers' whether related or not

for their children simply because they offer the first examples of leadership in one's life. That said, much of this research is dated, and a number of other factors can play a role in the development of an adult's leadership traits. Nevertheless, the interviewees consistently believed that exploring parental traits helped them better understand their clients' perspectives of authority.

Power Dynamics Including Reward and Punishment and Conflict Management

In addition to leadership traits, parents are the first and perhaps most impactful models of power dynamics. In fact, it can be argued that the parent(s) is the first boss the client ever had, and the family is the first organization the client ever belonged to. It is this notion of having power, control, and complete oversight that makes the parent the most powerful and very first template of leadership. This impact is much more conscious than the impact on leadership traits. The power dynamic–explored by many of the coaches, and including power-brokering, how power was used, who had it, and how it was distributed–were core areas of focus.

It is interesting to note, however, that the exploration of power was seldom addressed as such in the coaches' BI with clients. Often it was an inferred dynamic through stories of how family members were rewarded or punished: the parent responsible for delivering rewards or punishment held the power. Another facet of power represented through the parents was the level of democratization. In some client families, one parent might hold absolute power while in others the power might be shared between the parents. Likewise, some parents might encourage or allow challenges to their authority while others would eliminate any possibility of challenge.

"I worked with a client who once told me you never have just one boss. He grew up in a household where there were multiple tiers of authority, and depending on the nature of the request, you went to the relevant person. Having a sweetie after school was grandmother, getting a bad mark on a test went to dad".

The coaches also found a power dynamic link to the parents related to conflict management. The conflict management approach modelled by parents was often replicated in adulthood. How conflict was managed and resolved in families was the template for how to manage and resolve conflict with one's bosses, for example–since the first bosses in one's life are one's parents.

Although less prevalent in my study, followership–the ability to work effectively with leaders–could also be impacted by the family example. One coach found that a female client who grew up with a mother who had no power, no money, and no say in the decisions of the family struggled immensely with followership, particularly when working for a male leader.

Secondary research has linked Hierarchy issues to family-of-origin. Although other factors come into play, it is clear that the family is a powerful place of exploration for insight into leadership behavioural tendencies.

Isms of Your Family that Create the Normative Views on Behaviours

The Merriam-Webster Dictionary has a definition for an 'ism': 'manner of action or behaviour characteristic of a (specified) person or thing'. One might say, in other words, that an 'ism' is any type of action or behaviour that the family considers normal. In the secondary research, this topic is explored in different ways but using very different taxonomy. For example, areas explored include (1) how conflict is managed (Hovestadt et al., 1985; Glasgow et al., 1997; Aunola et al., 2000; Keller 2003; Hemming et al., 2012), (2) how power is distributed, and (3) the accepted levels of intimacy, openness to others, responsibility, and respect for others (Hovestadt et al., 1985; Manning, 2003; Mayseless, 2010; Hemming et al., 2012). These are all part of the formation of the isms of a family and how those isms can influence adult behaviour.

In the interviews, a significant ism explored by coaches includes emotional expression, particularly how attachment emotions such as love, happiness, and physical affection were expressed in the family. Equally relevant were the expressions of escape emotions such as anger, sadness, and fear. While emotional expression is an important element of a family's ism, emotions will be revisited in the dimension of Emotional Spectrum.

'Echoes' from Previous Generations

"As much as we look to parents and going into their patterns, it has a lot to do with what their own parents were going through as well. That's something that I see is not necessarily about what happened to us, it's also what happened to them. It's the exploration of the reinforcing factor".

Expert from Interview

Although certainly less prevalent than the influence of one's parents, philosophies from past generations can also influence the behaviours and actions of an individual–although not going back more than two to three generations. This is certainly the case for adults who grew up in multi-generational homes. Trauma, such as Holocaust survival, can also influence several generations of a family. Coaches might want to consider in their family-of-origin exploration the potential for multi-general influence on their clients.

Reinforcing Experiences with Other Authority Structures

Eventually, one leaves the family home and other sources of influence and experiences start to impact one's opinions of accepted behaviours and actions. Most telling are the early school years for clients. Suddenly, as a young child, the client is exposed to multiple models of what it means to be an adult through teachers. We start to see different ways of being, different ways of controlling, expressing, and using power. These experiences are then further compounded by the models a client may see through their friends' parents, then extracurricular coaches, and eventually other leadership models once the client enters the workforce. These rest-of-life experiences appear to either reinforce or challenge the original view of 'normal' from those early years. Described in different ways, it was the reference to life experiences beyond the family of origin that reinforced the clients' sense of self and how they should behave. Each life progression serves as a nuancing mechanism for the client of their own models and behaviours.

Coaches can have different opinions of the various stages (between the ages of 11 and 13 was a common suggestion) that make up these reinforcing structures. In any case, it is clear an exploration of family of origin alone will not suffice because much of what influences adult behaviour stems from reinforcing experiences outside the home. The secondary research on stage theory reflects this notion of changing maturity with progress of life experiences: the fact that people matured and evolved through stages across their lifespan as a result of a dynamic interaction between the inner self and the outer environment (Loevinger, 1979). Therefore, coaches should look for these moments of enforcing or challenging one's world view. Perspective and ways of being are non-static, constantly evolving processes, which is why (as we will see) that beyond parents, other stakeholders in the dimension of Hierarchy should be included, such as extended family, teachers, employers, and other authority figures.

Overall, it is suggested that the following ages tend to represent major milestones in stage shifts in templates of authority:
- Ages 5 – 7 when the client enters school and begins to see other families and teachers and therefore different models of adulthood.
- Ages 11 – 13 when a greater sense of 'I' versus 'others' is formed. The client begins to comprehend how the isms from their family of origin may contrast to the isms of other's families.
- Ages 14 – 17 when adolescence is in full bloom and the desire to (or not to) challenge the templates of leadership the client has been exposed to can begin to take shape.
- Age of independent living when the client begins modelling their own template of adulthood, particularly once they leave the family of origin.
- Age of caregiving responsibilities when the client either begins their own family and/or shifts roles with parent to primary caregiver.
- Age of parental transitions when the primary caregivers or significant hierarchy figures pass away.

Authority Expression in Organizational Life

Outside of family and school, the next most important context for Hierarchy in the life of a client relates to their professional life. It is the intersection of what has been taught and what the client chooses to express, though that may exist consciously and/or non-consciously. In the professional context, issues of leadership and power are at the forefront. What is clear from my study is the link between a client's views on leadership and power dynamics in their professional organizations and how it relates to their families of origin. For example, there were 47 references made to the term 'leadership' in the interviews. In examining these references, the correlation was that most discussions of leadership style eventually lead back to some form of BI, often relating styles of leadership to family-of-origin dynamics or, more specifically, how authority operated within the household. This is an important distinction because often narrative practices or any research related to BI and coaching sit outside the executive leadership realm and are often linked to life coaching. In fact, all of the interviewees thought that early childhood experiences with parents or primary caregivers, in particular, have a direct correlation with leadership behaviours demonstrated in adult life.

"Some clients have terrible histories that made them feel unsafe with people and so they split off and they keep their distance as leaders. I just really love to see these very intelligent senior leaders go down that pathway to understand why, often related to a parent. I think increasingly, we are in a position where we can act as a bridge to them to go off and do some of that work".

Ultimately, the data suggests that Hierarchy is a rich source of data that provides strong insight into the client and how they view, choose to use, and interact with their 'power' in organizational life. Secondary research likewise has made the link between biographical data, adult behaviour, and leadership performance. That said, these past studies that demonstrate a strong correlation data between the past and present are dated and lack serious evidence-based methodology. Moreover, none effectively outline a clear approach or framework with which to do an effective exploration of biographical data with clients (Mumford et al., 2009).

Overall Summary of Hierarchy

Two clear and distinct insights emerged from the data related to Hierarchy. The first was the influence of the family of origin, in particular parents, which was explored through four key dimensions: traits of parents, power dynamics, isms, and echoes from previous generations. The second insight was the evolution of those dynamics as the client went out into the world. The evolution included either a challenge to or reinforcement of those early templates at different life stages, particularly adolescence and early adulthood. Then the evolution continued as the client entered their professional careers and made conscious and non-conscious choices around the expression of their own leadership model. These real-life experiments created a cycle of adjustment that continues, in most cases, for the rest of their lives. This cycle creates a constant sense of adjustment back to the original template of leadership from family of origin. This overall dimension of Hierarchy is outlined in Figure 6.2.

BDMM - Hierarchy

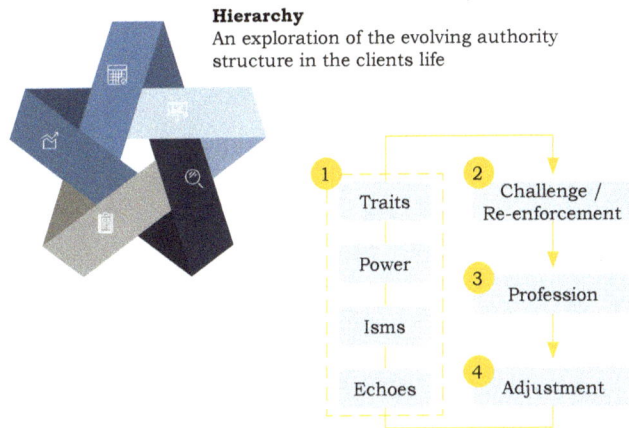

Figure 6.2 Four quadrants of exploration in Hierarchy

Peers

A strong majority of the interviewees made some reference to the term Peers (35 references). Other words to express this dynamic was siblings (34 references), friends/mates (30 references), cousins (11 references), colleagues (10 references), and classmates (7 references). What was so compelling about the exploration of this dimension is its relative importance in the majority of the interviews when it comes to influencing leadership tendencies, but rarely did it come up organically in BI until the coach specifically inquired into it, as this interviewee eloquently describes:

"It's funny, it's like thinking as a child, how did my bowl arrive at the table? Of course someone brought it there, but my experience begins with it just being there. I feel like that's what it is with siblings for most clients. They are there all time, very noisy, always in the conversation, yet we don't even mention them. It's funny and fascinating how I am seeing this. Of course, they [siblings] are the basis of conditioning, because without them, it wouldn't be such a societal condition, but it never occurs to clients to specifically call it out until asked".

The interviewees seemed to agree on the importance of peer-based dynamics, despite such dynamics not always being explicitly named by the client. Often the mention of Peers seems to awaken clients, who suddenly realize the influence of siblings or other Peers. The interviewees noted that this constant comparison with other children, siblings, classmates, or teammates was always in the background, but somehow it did not make it into the foreground unless some trauma occurred. There was this sense of it always being there and yet also some kind of unspoken code that often did not come into the discussion until adulthood. Yet the impact of Peers is widely felt on leadership tendencies in adulthood related to such things as innate sense of competition with others, desire for connectedness with others, and capacity for followership.

The lack of focus on Peer groups exists in the secondary research. Why does this dimension seem relevant in the exploration of the client through BI, yet seem undervalued as an intentional place of inquiry in secondary research? In terms of siblings, one reason is that there is not the same dynamism–the struggle for power, the challenges created in the relationship–among siblings as there is between children and their parents. Another rationale is that much of the research on siblings was based in large part on birth order, which has been through several cycles of debunking and proof (at least for particular tendencies).

The data from this research suggests there are two major considerations when exploring Peer dynamics:

1. Definition of what Peer groups are and how they are presented at various life stages.
2. How we transition within those groups,

which in turn informs leadership tendencies.

What Are Peer Groups?

"So much about how a person shows up in life is about how they are in relationships with others. These relationships are best demonstrated by how they are with their Peer groups and friends, and we often find quite echoing the relationships they held with their own siblings".

Expert from Interview

In family of origin, this dimension was often expressed as siblings and/or cousins. In school years, it was classmates, Peers and friends. In adulthood, or professional life, it often included colleagues and other co-workers at similar levels. Peers, it should be noted, did not necessarily mean 'those who are my equals'? Particularly within family of origin, siblings were not always treated and/or seen as equal. This notion of Peers over time does tend to move closer and closer to a sense of equals, but our earliest templates did not necessarily create this societal link.

Overall, there seemed to emerge this notion of three distinct Peer groups, which I have labelled as: inherited Peers, assumed Peers; and chosen Peers. Each of these Peer groups are then explored by their differences based on external and internal factors. External factors are the factors not related to the relationship, such as age, socio-economic factors, and perceived intelligence or capability. On the other hand, internal factors are based on elements such as connectedness and sense of competition–that is, factors that tended to influence behaviour.

Inherited Peers

Inherited Peers were those included in the family of origin, most often siblings and cousins. Clients did not have a choice in these relationships, which were created through family relationships. This Peer group is our first template of what it means to be in a relationship with others. It sets the tone for how we view being in relationships and the tendencies we adopt within them.

When examining this group of inherited Peers, in many ways, they were presumed to be similar on external factors such as socioeconomics, intelligence, and competence. (It should be noted these are often unfair presumptions based on intrinsic differences in capabilities between individuals and differences in socioeconomic means between families.) What this grouping really highlights is the societal conditioning on the desire for sameness, when sameness was often not the case.

In terms of internal factors, connectedness was assumed to be similar within the family, although, again, connectedness was perhaps an unfair assumption applied to all members of the family. What was considered variable was the degree of competition depending on the relationship dynamics and isms of the family.

Assumed Peers

What I called 'assumed' Peers were Peers from school (e.g., same class), sports, and other extra-curricular activities that a child might be involved with. Again, like with inherited Peers, there was no choice in these Peer groups, but rather they were assigned based on age or capability. This is where our inherited template begins to either be challenged or re-enforced by what we learned about being in relationship with others.

When considering the external factors, these Peers were deemed of similar age at school, although the factors were variable in the context of extra-curricular and sports activities, where one could have Peers at multiple age and socio-economic levels. There did seem to be an inference of a similar sense of intelligence and capability. In terms of internal factors, there was a sense of similar connectedness but variable competition–the sense of competition contingent on how a client might position themselves against their Peers.

Chosen Peers

This is the last Peer group formed but often the most impactful on leadership tendencies. Also known as the family you choose, these Peers are the ones the client intentionally chooses, such best friends and romantic partners, as well as close colleagues at work. On external factors, there seemed to be variability of age but similarity in socio-economic factors and intelligence and capability. In terms of internal factors, there was a sense of similar connectedness (after all, it was the family the client chose) and, again, variable degrees of competition. This Peer group tends to best personify the values and behavioural tendencies the client most believes in and enjoys being around. As the saying goes, 'Show me your friends and I'll show you your future.'

How We Explore Transition Within Peer Groups

"I'll check the relational aspect and how they shift. From siblings, to neighbours,

then school mates, and eventually adult relationships. These transitions, you know, moving from the home to how you relate and create relationships with the other kids, and each culture has a different transitional path. So, I will check what are the transitions that are in the culture that they come from. Eventually, the marital choices become fascinating. Who do they pick as their equal or not?"

Expert from Interview

One interesting perspective that emerged from the interviews was the idea of transitions and the insights those offered from a peer-based perspective. Each move from family to school to chosen tribe implied the acquisition of new and different Peers–mirroring in some ways the maturity stages of the client explored in the previous section on Hierarchy. In the secondary research, these Peer transitions might impact cognitive development–cognitive-developmental research suggests that an individual develops through interactions with society and Peers (Vygotsky, 1978; Tudge and Rogoff, 1999).

Of greater interest is the impact of Peer transitions on attachment–that is, the ability to create, form, and sustain relationships. It was this second dynamic that shifted the way the relationship or attachment dimension would be explored (as discussed later in this chapter under the dimension of Relationship).

Figure 6.3 outlines the overall dimension of Peers described in this section.

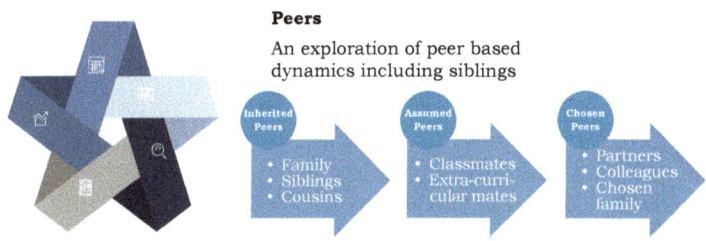

External Factors			
Age	Variable	Variable	Variable
Socio-economic	Similar	Variable	Similar
Intelligence / capability	Similar	Similar	Similar
Internal Factors			
Connectedness	Similar	Similar	Similar
Competition	Variable	Variable	Variable

Figure 6.3 Who are our Peers and what factors contribute to their definition?

Identity

"There is the aspect of the stories that one says about who they are and their place and their role in this world. Things like the unconscious rules about how the world works and therefore how I need to be within it. There is safety in knowing what I need to be but there is also the transition process, when the family Identity is challenged and the opportunity to define a new sense of self, emerges. It can be inherently and existentially terrifying".

Expert from Interview

In all the interviews, there was some form of exploration about Identity. While the terminology was often interchangeable between 'self' and 'Identity' the definition was consistently the same: Identity (or self) refers to *the stories we tell ourselves about who we are.* Identity was the third most-referenced dimension in the study, only following Hierarchy and emotions. What makes Identity such an integral part of BI is because it informs so much about who the client is at both a conscious and non-conscious level as well as at an aspirational level. This idea of who we were taught to be, who we learned and choose to be, and ultimately who we are aspiring to be in the future.

Through this research, the data collected identified that Identity had three component elements or stages:

1. 'Inherited' Identity
2. 'Constructed' Identity
3. the 'Transitional' stage (the journey between Inherited and Constructed Identity)

We explore each of these below.

Inherited Identity

"I think it's important to know how Identity was formed [for the client], and it often goes back to the family, early relationships, cultural perspective, rooted in the past about who they should be".

Expert from Interview

Inherited Identity is built from elements attached to one's sense of self not by choice, but through elements such as religion, race expectations, socio-economic expectations, and the values that governed the family of origin. These elements are often described as parts of 'who I am supposed to be'.

Inherited Identity is the sense of Identity established in the early years, often through family of origin. Often, the components of this inherited Identity can sit within the non-conscious, such as implied religious expectations. In Asia, children are often streamed into groups based on their academic performance, and this academic performance label will stay with them well into their professional careers.

Overall, inherited Identity seemed to have several drivers:

- System-driven identifiers – race, culture, religion, language, country of birth, and socio-economic factors.
- Behaviour-driven drivers – the acceptable forms of behaviour in the family, such as gender role expectations. Gender and sexuality roles often stemmed from this driver.
- Responsibility-driven drivers – the responsibilities and expected achievements based on one's role in the family.

Important to the inquiry of inherited Identity is the degree of safety the clients feel within these expectations. Related and equally important is the degree of success the client had in meeting these expectations. If the client was able to find personal success and safety within the boundaries of this Inherited |Identity, the journey through Transitional and Constructed Identity may be less pronounced or traumatic. However, in cases where clients either rejected their Inherited Identity, felt unsecure, or could not meet the expectations, then the journey through Transitional and Constructed may be much more pronounced and material.

Constructed Identity

"I worked with a lady who was a regional vice-president of a large software company. I asked her, who would you be if you weren't regional vice-president. She looked at me and said, nobody. She was someone who created a world where she had power and used that power to broker how others should treat her, ultimately how she deemed her own Identity and self-worth".

Expert from Interview

Constructed Identity implies having full agency over the elements that define your expected behaviours. The elements of constructed Identity are actively chosen by the client and included as a part of their being. Constructed Identity is often the outcome of the renegotiation and reconstruction of the self that the client is choosing to be, rather than the self that they were told to be via their family of origin. The seduction of these constructed identities can be so compelling that often we do not see their power over us. The way we want to be perceived becomes the way we want to perceive ourselves. When confronted with behaviours that are not in congruence, we see how the client perceives themselves and the elements of Constructed Identity, which can often cause deep pain and is often the source of some form of trauma.

The importance of this dimension is undeniably supported by the secondary research with meaning and Identity as foundational to all coaching. (Bush et al., 2013).

The Transitional Identity

The third component of Identity is the transitioning of Identity between the Inherited and Constructed identities. In this transitional stage, sense-making seems to actively adjust as life events emerge. This adjustment can sometimes take the form of polarities. For example, a person raised in a household with constant conflict may be used to conflict; some, however, will reject this inherited Identity in favour of the polar opposite, seeking to avoid conflict at all costs. Conflict avoidance is part of who they are. A traumatic event can likewise lead individuals to transition to a different stage in their Identity.

The launch of a transitional Identity stage is often a non-conscious process. Feeling safe (e.g., normal) non-consciously reinforces their behaviour and sense of Identity, and thus there is no reason to seek to change the status quo. However, when the feeling of safety is compromised, depending on the internal sense of power the client may feel, the behaviours and sense of Identity can be challenged. When a client is in the transitional stage, it is important to define the ideal Constructed Identity. Helping the client bring these elements and expectations to life will help ground the client through the journey and help the client gain some sense of agency during the transition phase.

Overall Summary of Identity

Identity appears to flow through perceived stages–inherited to transitional to constructed identities–between the stories we tell ourselves about whom we should be versus whom we choose to be.

The journey through the four stages is driven by a cycle of (1) no awareness (or non-questioning), (2) critical awareness of difference (3) judgement of differences, and finally (4) re-construction of ideal self, as summarized in Figure 6.4.

This cycle begins with awareness on the

need for change. As mentioned, awareness can come from many places including lack of safety in expectations, rejection of expectations, or awareness that there can be other models of Identity that feel different to anything experienced in Inherited Identity.

Through this awareness, the client then moves into stage 2 of judgement about these differences. These judgements can hold the risk for trauma, especially if related to elements of expected behaviour that the client felt little to no agency over. Clients must thus proceed delicately as they transition through the process of evaluating what this foundationally means to who they are.

Moving past judgement needs a deep level of integration work to then create the possibility of what could exist to replace these old expectations: this is stage 3, called re-construction. This is the stage in which the possible Constructed Identity is formed.

Finally, once integrated within this stage (which maps to the macro Transitional stage), clients move into the 4th stage of non-questioning, until the next Identity crisis emerges. For some, clients can cycle through these stages often, whereas others will have done very little movement between inherited to constructed (e.g., who they are looks very similar to who they were expected to be).

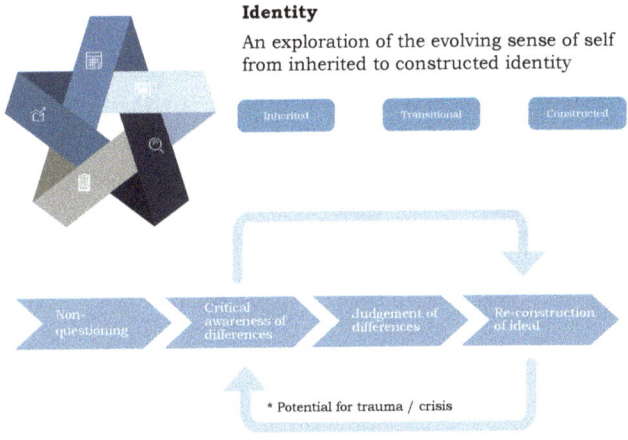

Figure 6.4 The progression of Identity

Context

I think it is very important to consider the social realm [context] because people don't exist in a vacuum. Anything they do is going to have an impact on the systems that they sit in and has been informed by the systems from which they came. So, I think, one of the things that I particularly think about when working with clients is that you cannot ignore the broader context of their lives.

When working with clients through BI, coaches cannot ignore the diversity of experiences and backgrounds of their clients–the broader *context* of their lives–that will greatly influence their meaning making. Culture and race, socio-economic background, spiritual beliefs, and age or generation were identified in the interviews as four key contextual drivers that coaches must deliberately consider during the BI process.

Culture and Race Drivers

Culture and race place different pressures and expectations on clients–pressures and expectations that coaches must understand as part of their coaching work. Coaching and coaching psychology research has focused on systemic race and ethnicity issues. Contextual factors, however, are not explicitly clear because the impact of such elements can often occur at the non-conscious level. Coaches must be able to discern, for example, what, in an Asian context, a Malaysian Muslim would consider strength in leadership as compared to a Filipino Catholic. These culture and race drivers can be difficult to uncover if clients themselves are not aware of the impact of these inferred ways of being has on their own leadership tendencies. As such, making explicit during BI the inquiry into the race and cultural drivers that influenced the client's upbringing helps both the coach and client understand what might inform how the client behaves. The focus on how these drivers enable and/or hinder their perspective taking and tendencies is essential to the discovery.

The secondary research on this topic is insufficient. Passmore (2010) suggests that effective coaching requires the consideration of the diversity of the client as a theme and that coaches have a responsibility to understand their own cultural heritage before assisting other people: a lack of such understanding could hinder effective intervention. Roth suggests coaching is there to raise awareness of cultural competence in both clients and the coaches working with them who are from other cultural backgrounds (Roth, 2017). And while there are references in the coaching and coaching psychology literature about systemic race and ethnicity issues, they are primarily insights borrowed from the social sciences and explore common themes around negotiating identities, privilege, blind spots, and systemic discrimination (Rankin-Wright et al., 2017). However, none of the secondary research actually provides a framework on how to do this type of exploration.

Socio-economic drivers

"As children, we don't necessarily have a sense of enough. So, it's delineated from what our parents tell us is enough or not. Eventually, over time, we develop greater self-awareness, based on social normative behaviour in our reference groups. Whether that's family, our school system, or socio-economic status, there is a different philosophy for each level and over time, we decide if that is fair, enough, and just".

Expert from Interview

Socio-economic dynamics from childhood can play a role in adulthood. Slightly more than half of the interviewees said they explicitly explored this issue, while the other half explored this issue more implicitly, if at all. Coaches can explore through BI how much of a role socio-economic background plays within the Context of current dynamics and goals. Often the sense of have and have-not as a child can inform the values that drive us in adulthood. There was some very interesting exploration within the interviews of what it meant to be a second- or third-generation affluent family versus growing up as second- or third-generation poor–and how their different upbringings impacted the way these clients navigated life in adulthood. What was not clear was the causation and/or patterning that emerges (as all client case studies were diverse and unable to make consistent conclusions). Nevertheless, the exploration of social-economic drivers was material to some clients.

The secondary research on socioeconomic factors and coaching focuses on accessibility– the role of affluence in enabling individuals to benefit from coaching. This is not relevant to this research because socioeconomic factors are being considered in the Context of a client's life experiences and how those experiences impact their meaning making.

Spiritual Drivers

A majority of the coaches interviewed approached this contextual factor by asking, 'Are you a spiritual person?' or 'Does spirituality play a role in your life?' This line of questioning is felt more appropriate than more specific questions about the client's religion because the client can choose how much or little they want to divulge. The data from the interviews was mixed on its materiality. For those clients who were spiritual and chose to reveal this data, the link between leadership tendencies, values, and behaviours was highly correlated and therefore material. In other cases, the choice to shift ideological beliefs or to move away from certain religious practices also showed materiality. However, equally, there was no evidence that a lack of spiritual practice or religiosity had any direct impact on behaviour tendencies. Therefore, the conclusion was that the exploration of this area in BI was one to give the client the opportunity to share its materiality in whatever way felt important to them and relevant to their goals.

The secondary research into religious traditions and spirituality is vast and complex. The most relevant was how spirituality is often explored in coaching to provide a greater understanding of the beliefs that drive the client (Elliott, 2010). Elliott proposes a six-pronged inquiry that explores beliefs though rituals, experience, social structure, texts, stories and myths, ethics, and symbols. This provides a framework that helps coaches become aware of the religious beliefs or personal spiritual beliefs of the client, which might have an impact on the client's leadership. Elliott's conclusion is supported by Rosinski, who argues that an exploration of spirituality and religion can provide insights on both external cultural characteristics that the client may exhibit and prefer, and internal characteristic such as values and basic assumptions/fundamental beliefs (Rosinski, 2011).

Age and Generational Drivers

Few of the interviewees explored the roles of age and generation with their clients. There are perhaps implicit and generally accepted implications of different generations (as one interviewee explained, 'Baby boomers see the world in a different Context than Gen Y'). However, understanding the Context of the geopolitical and social landscape can be valuable in the Context of generational differences. For example, gender roles and identification can be highly influenced by the generation from which the client was raised. One interviewee who does significant work with the Singapore government believed that the generation who grew up with former Prime Minister Lee Kuan Yew at the helm of the country (he led Singapore's independence and governed for more than 30 years) had a very different perspective on leadership than the newer generation of leaders.

Another interviewee noted that today's generational drivers drew on influences that did not exist before:

"Influence goes beyond the family of origin, beyond the world that we live in. If you were a child in the past 20 years, you grew up in an age of digitization and online social media. There was never really the

segregation between you and the bubble of where you grew up versus the outside world. As a child, you watched families on TV in America and borrowed some of those cultural norms. I see kids born and raised in Singapore with American accents. We can no longer think in the geographical-bounded terms we once did".

Overall Summary of Context

Within each of these Context drivers (culture and race, socio-economic background, spiritual beliefs, and age or generation drivers), there is a degree of family and societal expectations, either implicit or explicit, that fundamentally fuel behaviour implications for the client.

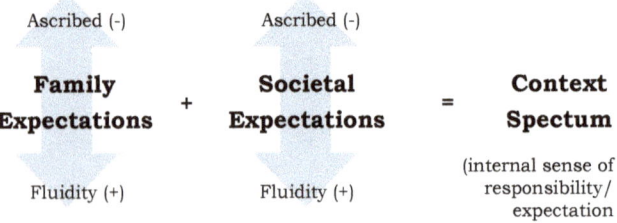

Figure 6.5 The Context Spectrum

These expectations and one's response to these expectations can be placed on a 'Context spectrum' based on the internal sense of responsibility and/or expectations a client feels, given their background. This spectrum ranges from 'ascribed' drivers–for example, what it means to be a person of colour in a given country, or to be part of a minority religious sect in a highly religious country–to 'fluidity', whereby the client makes their own sense of materiality and meaning based on their personal version of reality.

As described in each of the individual Context drivers already discussed, there is limited research related to these topics–the one exception being the impact of age and generations, which has been studied extensively in academic research. Managing the generational workforce is only one example of an area of study in this field. There is a growing awareness, however, that perhaps generational differences have been overstated. Perhaps the most relevant concept to be drawn from the research is the idea of recognizing the differences between coach and client in the inferences they may be making about each other based on generational similarities and/or differences.

Emotional Spectrum

Working with emotions was the most explored topic within the interviews. There were two major ways the interviewees explored emotional data. First, they explored how emotional data was expressed and processed within the client's family of origin and how this was enforced or challenged as the client progressed through life. This ultimately informed the template for the client's spectrum of emotional expression and how that informed leadership tendencies. The second was actually working with emotional expression during the session itself to process what might be happening for the client on a non-conscious level.

The significance of this exploration expressed in the interviews is re-enforced in the secondary research on this topic. Research suggests that helping the client engage with emotions in the coaching process helps coaches to be aware of how a client progresses or is hindered by emotions, and the impact of such progress or lack of progress on a client's ability to achieve sustainable change (O'Broin and Palmer, 2019). The research also highlights critical moments of intense emotion during coaching that reveal pivotal shifts for the client (Day et al., 2008). (Wilson, 2004). Finally, as suggested by Bachkirova and Cox (2007b), most academic research focuses on using emotions to

(1) understand attitudes at work, (2) to engage in and with the coaching process; and (3) for the coach to help the client engage with and express emotions.

In examining the emotions-related data from the interviews, my analysis revealed three core areas:

- Which emotions matter?
- Emotions as the 'gatekeeper' to what may be happening non-consciously.
- The driver of action and/or behaviour.

Which Emotions Matter?

"I will often use the word experience as a generic word for wanting to talk about emotion. Easier to let emotions begin to be apparent, rather than start naming them up front. Also important to reflect this is the kind of range of emotions that we're going to be talking about, and how emotions mixed together to create feelings".

Expert from Interview

As described in Chapter 2, Brown and Dzendrowskyj (2018) explore emotions as attachment-based (love/trust, excitement/joy) or escape-based (sadness, shame, disgust, anger, fear) and startle/surprise–what is called 'curiosity' in this research. According to the data from this research, one's comfort with expressing attachment-based emotions has its roots in early life where open expressions of love and joy were encouraged–although it is true that such early life experiences can also lead to an avoidance or fear of pain. Nevertheless, the soul strives for attachment-based emotions and a greater move towards this is desirable.

For about half of the interviewees, the emotion or feeling of curiosity often came up as a place of exploration for the coach. Coaches used their own curiosity to dig deeper into a line of inquiry, which often resulted in interesting insights. Coaches also used curiosity as a tool for the clients themselves to go deeper. Thus, curiosity gave both the coach and the client the capacity to explore and unearth things that they might have missed (a realization reflected in the work of Brown and Dzendrowskyj (2018)).

While attachment-based emotions and curiosity had their place in coaching, the emotions explored most frequently with clients were escape emotions (sadness, shame, disgust, anger, fear). Coaches explored such emotions in one of three ways:

1. by unlocking pain from the past and/or family of origin;

2. by tracing the root cause in the present; or
3. to enable discussions on issues that were difficult to explore.

The appearance of escape emotions was a signal for the coaches to dig deeper and find the causes in the past of these emotions. As one interviewee said, *'When sadness comes into the room, tracing that back to the past and where sadness came from helps us see why it's here today'*. Another insight from the data concerned difficulty with expressing certain emotions, which, as opposed to easy-to-express emotions, indicated that some level of pain sat in the non-conscious and required addressing. Another interesting perspective that emerged from the data was the difference between inferred and expressed emotions–of particular interest given the number of coaches working in Asia among the interviewees. Some believed emotions were deeply suppressed, while others said escape emotions rather than attachment emotions were often more expressed in family of origin. The difference, according to one interviewee reflecting on these two viewpoints, was likely the sense of inferred feelings (e.g., knowing you are loved, even if it is not said or expressed in a hug or kiss) versus expressed feelings.

Emotions as the 'Gatekeeper' to What May Be Happening Non-consciously

"When we explore what is really happening in the client, it is not a thinking system. Thinking is just telling us a post-hoc story of what the brain already knows. It's the story house of experience. What we want to uncover is what does the brain already know? This inquiry is attributed to emotions".

Expert from Interview

The relationship between emotions and the non-conscious was evident in all the interviews. Exploring emotions, according to one interviewee, allowed the coach to dig *'layer by layer into what's really going on.'* By exploring through emotions to what sits under the surface, the coach and client slowly bring non-consciousness into consciousness through emotional language and somatic experience.

The somatic experience of emotions was also an important aspect of emotions as gatekeepers to the non-conscious. Emotional expression requires accessing language that may be unfamiliar or uncomfortable for some clients–sometimes based, as noted above, on early childhood lessons of whether or not it was appropriate to outwardly express emotions and sometimes based on societal expectations. As one interviewee explained, the conditioning that society (or family of origin) places on the appropriateness of expressing certain emotions such as anger makes us unaware that we are feeling it; for that reason, connecting to the body and what is happening in the body can be a window into these unconsciously suppressed emotions. Thus, in the words of one interviewee, *'the unconscious becomes conscious by going through a little journey, starting in the body, walking past our history and pain, to something new'*.

These somatic expressions have some grounding in secondary research, notably in theory and research from neuroscience, interpersonal neurobiology, developmental psychology, and attachment theory (Gus et al., 2015).

Emotions as the Driver of Action or Behaviour Change

"Science is telling us all behaviour is the result of the way emotions got connected to experience, and then we happen to attach words to them. So, what I'm directing people's attention to all the time is to try and track the emotional flow and what the underlying

> *emotions are. I'm very keen on hyphenating the word emotions into E-motions to keep reminding us that emotions are the drivers to behaviours".*
>
> Expert from Interview

The idea of emotions being the driver of behaviour change or creating new behaviours was shared by several of the interviewees. As one interviewee suggested, nothing can in fact sustainably change without some form of non-conscious access, and emotions offer (as described above) this access. For another interviewee, emotions were the source of healing required in order to shift into new behaviours. Emotions, according to this interviewee, invite the *'shadow to appear, shine a light on it, and ultimately heal it so that those emotional triggers go away and we can give light to something new'*.

Summary of Emotional Spectrum

The data on the use of emotions in coaching yields two distinct implications. One is the link between the type of emotion and the client's ability to be able to operate at an optimal leadership capacity. Researching a client's past for the origins of emotions can reveal the source of behavioural patterns in the present.

The other insight is the use of emotions as the anchoring element to what exists in the non-conscious, which has been termed 'Emotions into Consciousness Journey', as illustrated in Figure 6.6.

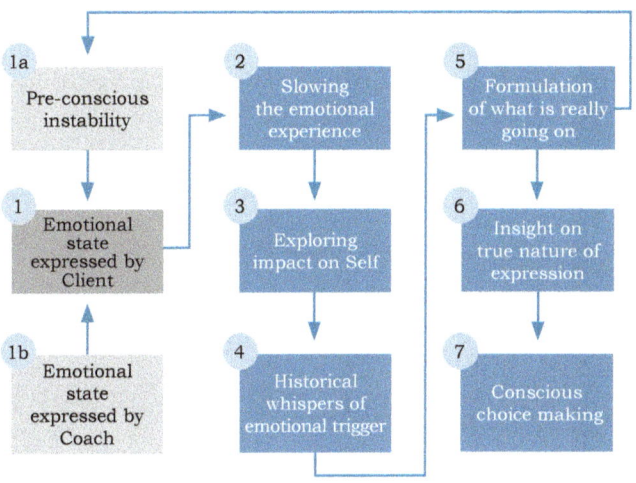

Figure 6.6 Emotions into Consciousness Journey

Emotions into Consciousness Journey

The Emotions into Consciousness journey unfolds as follows:

Step 1. Pre-conscious instability leads to an emotional state expressed (perhaps consciously or non-consciously) by the client or recognized and expressed first by the coach. The exploration in Step 1 is to name the state being expressed and what may have sparked that state.

Step 2. The next step is to slow the state down by identifying the experience of it. This may involve a somatic expression within the body. The client fully embodies the emotional state, what it feels like and where they feel it in the body, thus bringing into consciousness the experience of the state.

Step 3. This step explores the impact of the emotional state. For some, sitting with the discomfort of the emotional state can be quite triggering.

Step 4. Step 3 can very quickly lead to Step 4, where the coach helps the client explore the historical context of the emotional state. For example, a client may be feeling anger or sadness but due to lessons of the past, may be reticent to explore such feelings. The coach must help the client ignore the templates of the past and focus on why the client is feeling that state in

The Six Dimensions of Biographical Inquiry

the present, which can finally lead to what may genuinely be going on.

Step 5. Time to move back to the present and to help formulate an approach or understanding of what is really triggering the client. One way is to return to Step 1, or what I call Step 1a because the entire process begins again but this time to identify the core driver. The alternative is to move the discussion into Step 6, which is the insight into the true nature of the emotional expression.

Step 6. In this step, the client and coach move beyond the act of feeling the trigger to focus on what can be done to resolve it. This attitude enables the client to into the final Step 7.

Step 7. This is the active choice-making step, when the client is no longer subject to the emotion but is instead able to make conscious choices.

Relationship as the Anchoring Driver Across All Dimensions of the BDMM© Model

The final dimension of the BDMM© framework is the concept of attachment and/or Relationship–a dimension explored in all the interviews. Analysis of the data revealed that Relationship was at the heart of each and every dimension, yet also merited consideration as a standalone dimension. Relationship dynamics based on safety, agency, and expression were explored implicitly. More explicit exploration of relationships occurred around topics of adolescence and the choosing of friendships and lovers. In general, however, disentangling Relationship from the dimensions was both a challenge but also essential due to the complexity of the inquiry.

Foundationally, the exploration of Relationship was to understand the client's capacity for connection, in particular, connectedness and disconnection to self, people, context, and things. The core driver of insights about relationships came from the following areas:

- How to create and be in relationship with those with power (related to Hierarchy dimension)
- How to create and be in relationship with equals (related to Peer dimension).

- How to create and be in relationship with self (related to Identity dimension).
- How to create and be in relationship with a greater system context, such as family, marriage/partnership, society, parenthood, and assets (related to Context dimension).

Table 6.1 summarizes how in the data Relationship was explicitly or implicitly explored within each dimension.

Table 6.1 Explicit and implicit drivers with biographical dimensions of meaning making

Dimension		Nature of exploration
Hierarchy	Explicit	Relationship with parents, teachers, and other hierarchal figures, and the degree of closeness and comfort within authority and higher power structures.
	Implicit	The amount of safety, agency, and self-expression expressed by the client within those relationships.
Peers	Explicit	Relationship with Peers through various stages of life from siblings (if applicable), into friendships, romantic partnerships, and professional colleagues; the shift in the relationship between inherited and chosen family.
	Implicit	The amount of safety, agency, and self-expression felt by the client within these relationships.

Identity	Explicit	The sense of self-love, self-confidence, and self-acceptance.
	Implicit	How the client felt accepted by others, which led to acceptance of self.
Context	Explicit	Sense of community, extended connection into a greater system of belonging beyond the family.
	Implicit	Relationship to status and classification (Does the client truly belong anywhere or self-identify with a larger sense of society?).
Emotional Spectrum	Explicit	The ease with which the client can connect, communicate, and express felt emotions.
	Implicit	The amount of safety and agency felt by the client within the expression of the emotions. (Is it safe to be sad, angry shameful, happy?).

The importance of a client's ability to create and sustain relationships with others has strong theoretical foundations in the secondary research on attachment theory. In the context of BDMM©, the application of attachment theory to leadership is the most relevant (Drake, 2009). For example, research has linked secure attachment dynamics to effective leadership, including a greater tendency to be nominated as leaders, to adopt more empowering leadership styles, and achieve positive outcomes (Mayseless, 2010). Furthermore, relationship competence is considered by the research to be a more crucial criterion with which to measure leadership effectiveness than technical competence and organizational experience (Manning, 2003).

The third focus in the exploration of the dimension of Relationship, beyond (1) the client's capacity for connectedness and disconnection to self, people, context and things, and (2) the explicit and implicit insights into behavioural tendencies in adulthood (outlined earlier in the chapter), is to (3) understand how our preferred attachment styles impact our leadership tendencies.

By examining clients across the Avoidance-Anxiety matrix (see Figure 6.7), we can see how early childhood patterns inform our tendencies, which helps the coach understand which levers to further explore in order to create behavioural change. The avoidance spectrum gives the coach insights into how willing the client is to lean into the difficult conversation and address the issues directly (or not). The anxiety spectrum gives the coach insight into the degree to which relationships cause anxiety in the client. In cases of low avoidance and low anxiety, the client holds secure attachment tendencies, which means they likely have many healthy relationships and likely minimal conflict. If the client is high avoidance and low anxiety, the client tends to demonstrate dismissive attachment tendencies, which means they can seem uncaring or unwilling to address conflict and relationship challenges. If the client is high avoidance and high anxiety, the client likely holds a fearful style, which means they likely seek avoidance, particularly when there is any perceived conflict, and generally find relationship dynamics to cause significant distress. Finally, if the client is low avoidance and high anxiety, they can succumb to preoccupied tendencies that, again, carries a high cost to the client and to those around them as issues are not often dealt with in a direct manner.

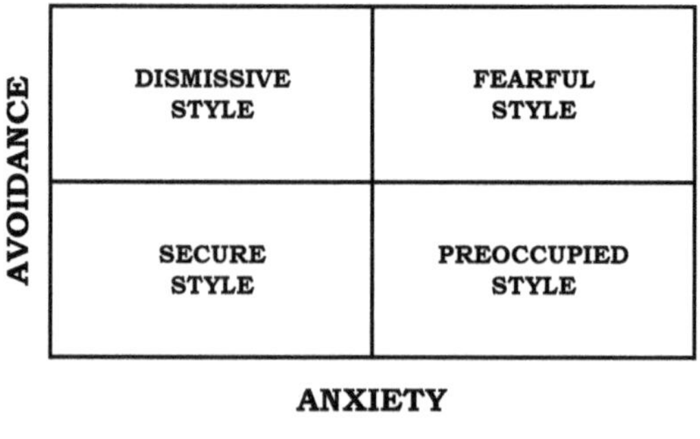

AVOIDANCE	**DISMISSIVE STYLE**	**FEARFUL STYLE**
	SECURE STYLE	**PREOCCUPIED STYLE**

ANXIETY

Figure 6.7 The Avoidance-Anxiety Matrix.

CHAPTER 7

What Biographical Inquiry Tells Us

Biographical inquiry (BI) is more than listening to the stories of the client. The coach and client must mine the stories for the insights they offer for the purposes of coaching. Those insights come from both the coach's interpretation of the narratives but more importantly from how the client interprets and interacts with the stories. How do the stories inform who the client is now and how do they deal with their current challenges? How does the client make meaning from the stories? How much power do these stories still have on the client response patterns? And more fundamentally, how can these stories be re-interpreted to create new meaning in order to achieve the goals they have set out for themselves? These types of questions form a key part of the BI process.

This chapter first reviews what the six BI dimensions infer about leadership behaviours. Identifying these inferences–see the framework below–was based on the topics explored in each interview and further expanded and developed based on the secondary research from psychology, coaching psychology, and applied sciences.

The chapter then introduces the concept of stages, or shifts, that occur in the telling of biographical data based on the client's agency towards the stories. Understanding from which stage the client is describing and interacting with the narrative allows the coach and client to interpret how much capacity the client has for change, re-interpretation, and new meaning making that ultimately impacts behaviours.

What the Dimensions Infer about Leadership Behaviours

How does the past relate to current leadership behaviour or tendencies? What we know from the extensive secondary research in psychology is that it is the holy trinity of family of origin, attachment dynamics, and identity that often have the strongest and most significant impact on adult behaviours. In addition, they are often the source of dysfunction and trauma in adulthood. The research in this study revealed not only how this holy trinity relates to key leadership behaviours, but how all the dimensions inform a more dynamic portrait of the client. More importantly, in several areas where there was limited secondary research, this research becomes the foundation and beginning first steps into building the collective knowledge.

Additionally, this is the first empirical study done relating to the past, that is 100% with an organizational lens. As all the interviewees practiced in an organizational setting, all the research was mapped to leadership tendencies and challenges, and all the work done in these coaching relationships revealed insights into the client's past which led to real and measurable behaviour change in the sponsoring organizations.

The six dimensions of BDMM©, therefore, is the first effective map to help identify and organize the insights on leadership behaviour and tendencies that can be inferred from the narratives of the past. These narratives of a client, might, for example, clearly indicate that client's ease or difficulty in relationship with authority figures, or their emulation of the leadership styles of authority figures to which they have been exposed.

A fascinating output of this research was how nature versus nurture for that client comes to life in their current context. Let's highlight, for example, how a psychometric assessment may be a very useful tool to understand how a leader shows up in an organizational context. In addition, the psychometric may also provide their predictive response patterns in certain situations. However, what we do not get with psychometrics is any reliable data on how to actually influence change. As most psychometrics are based on the five-factor model of personality, one cannot simply change personality traits in order to show up differently. Even more important, we do not know the why or where these traits come from. While some may be inherent (or nature), many are learned and therefore the implication is that they can be unlearned and re-learned. By going through the past and understanding why these leaders do what they do, and the meaning they make (either consciously or non-consciously), coaches know how the source information to help a client can map a path to sustainable change.

As shown in Table 7.1, analysis of the interviews ultimately led to a comprehensive overview of the leadership behaviours to be inferred from each of the dimensions.

It is important to note that the themes in the table above reflect insights into the client's leadership behaviours and tendencies in the present. BI does not purport to predict the future; however, what BI can do is provide a valuable formulation approach in which the coach and client can make hypotheses together about what may be happening on a much deeper level for the client, often in the non-conscious, and give the client access to data that may support a sustainable shift–data often unreachable without the insights from BI.

Table 7.1 Leadership behaviours based on each dimensions within BDMM©

Dimension	Leadership behaviours related to the dimension
Hierarchy	• Leadership styles as they relate to templates clients have been exposed to (often parents, teachers, mentors, bosses) • Leadership tendencies as it relates to need for power, agency, and control • A client's overall relationship to power–how they wield it, how they are impacted by it and how comfortable they are to have it • How a client relates and is in relationship with authority and other power structures • How a client relates power to control, particularly in hierarchical relationships • Exhibiting highly controlled versus distributed leadership style
Peers	• A client's preferred tendencies and role within group and team dynamics • Collaboration style with others of equal power and in group settings • Ability to share and distribute power and leadership • Willingness and degree of followership • Degree of inclusion/acceptance desired by others and the innate degree of belonging a client may desire or aspire to • Sense of competitiveness versus collegial dynamics with others
Identity	• How the client fundamentally defines who they are, what they stand for, and how they want to show up in the world • Degree of self-awareness and self-expression • How they project confidence and inner self-belief • The client's self-preservation/self-protection tendencies • The ease in expressing, communicating, and demonstrating executive presence • Driver of mindset, adaptability, and resilience • The source data for most inner turmoil the client may be feeling (the existential conflict between who I should be - who I want to be – who I aspire to be).

Context	- A client's fundamental sense of right, wrong, and fairness
- Relationship with societal expectations that are culturally, religiously, geographically, or gender defined
- Acceptance and appreciation of diversity
- Interaction styles with perceived 'insiders' versus 'outsiders/others'
- Sense of belonging to a larger system/dynamics
- Curiosity about the unknown
Relation-ship	- Capacity for connection–connectedness and disconnection to self, people, context and things
- Engagements, nature, and style of interaction with others
- Ability to create trust and psychological safety
- How to relate to others
- Source data for team dynamics
Emotional Spectrum	- Non-conscious patterning of behaviours/tendencies that are expressed through emotional data
- How the client can express and react to a full spectrum of emotions, particularly escape (anger, shame, sadness, fear) and attachment-based emotions (love, joy, happiness)
- Degree of integration as a leader
- Emotional maturity/intelligence
- Emotional expressiveness and vulnerability
- Overall sense of resilience

How to Interpret the Data from BDMM©

"The exploration of the stories is where it all begins, but it's only one part. Holding the experiences as objects to explore becomes an almost real-time meaning-making exercise where the client moves from reliving the story to being in a dance with it. Some stories will still hurt, some stories flow

> *through like energy, and others get caught up on one thing or another. You begin to see a picture form of what elements of the past are still playing out".*

Expert from Interview

In more than half of the interviews, the interviewees introduced the concept of stages or phases of the BI process based on the increasing level of agency that clients gain with regards to the story. In other words, to what extent does the narrative have a psychological or emotional hold on the client? At one end, the story or memory will still have a significant impact on how the client behaves or thinks; at the other end of the agency spectrum, the client has moved beyond the self-narrative, which no longer holds power or acts as an anchor but acts instead as a reference point.

This concept of stages is borrowed from the work of Kegan (1985), who described meaning making through a subject–object perspective. This perspective examines whether clients, as they are telling their stories, are *subject* to the experience (e.g., reliving trauma over and over again non-consciously), or instead, are able to keep stories at a psychological distance and view them objectively. Interviewees described this objective perspective variably as *'hold [the past] to object'*, 'can they see it?', and *'able to recognize the pain of it but not be subject to it anymore'*. The process of being able to hold the experience as object is a good sign, according to another interviewee, in that the client has the psychological or emotional resources to go into the past, including revisiting past trauma, and not require counselling or therapy.

Based on the clients' telling of the stories, and the meaning making that clients were extracting from the past events in question, the interviewees did not envision this spectrum of increasing client agency as a continuum, but consisting instead of several stages.

In the first stage, which was referenced in all the interviews, the client was *subject* to a narrative or story, as described by this coach from the perspective of a client:

"It's important to understand what I'm subject to. What I can't see. I haven't got perspective on it. It's not known to me. I might see the outcomes or the ramifications of a pattern of thinking or an assumption or whatever. But I can't see the cause-ology. I just know what I am experiencing takes hold of me".

About half of the interviewees referenced a second stage of agency, which was being able to hold the experience as an *observation* or *reflection*, as described by this interviewee:

> *"Important to see if they can differentiate within their experiences, from what they had agency over, [and] what systems and structures existed which they may not have any control over, but that affect them anyway. How do they make sense of their experiences now? And how might that affect what they do today and in the future?"*

About a quarter of the interviewees alluded to a third and final *transcendence* stage, described as follows:

> *"The experience becomes a root for expression. A root for having conversations and a scaffold to help myself and others understand and find a way through a problem they're struggling with. The experience becomes a language that one could work with. Not to constrain, but to expand. A subtle self-development theory or approach for enabling us to consider what matters in this experience, what still needs exploring and what elicits surprise".*

In the secondary research, little evidence links the three stages described above (subject to a narrative; observation and reflection; transcendence) to leadership effectiveness (Lawrence, 2017), although some studies have found a strong correlation between clients subject to their narratives and poor leadership (Lawrence,

2017; Eigel and Kuhnert, 2005; Strang and Kuhnert, 2009). However, Bachkirova and Cox (2019) applied the stages specifically to coaching, building on the work of Berger (2012), who developed a constructive-developmental coaching approach in which the exchange between coach and client enables a coach to gauge the stage the client may be in. This exchange can then spark within the client an effort to break free from the narrative, moving on to a next, greater agency stage. Specifically, as coaches listen to the detail and level of description of the story itself, they form a vivid picture of the stage in which the story is described; they can then infer the impact of that particular stage on the client's leadership behaviours.

Blending the leadership traits explored in each dimension with the three emerging stages just described led to three levels within each of the six dimensions, as shown in Figure 7.1. Let's examine each of these levels more closely.

Unfolding

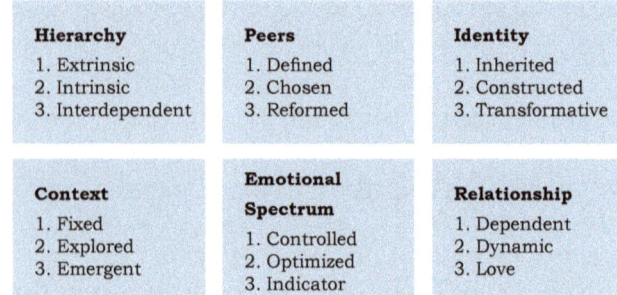

Figure 7.1. The journey of stages within biographical dimensions of meaning making

Hierarchy

The three key stages within this dimension are: **extrinsic, intrinsic,** and **interdepend**ent. At the extrinsic stage, leadership behaviours and tendencies emerge as a reaction to the external environment. Decisions are thus made as a response to external events that clients do not believe are controllable.

When clients move into the intrinsic stage, they begin to sense that they have more power or agency over events. The external dynamics still exist, but now the client is able to internalize them to make meaning and more informed decisions.

The final stage is interdependent, in which the

client believes they have an equal role in both creating the external dynamics and responding to the outcomes of these dynamics. There is less differentiation between what is external and what is internal; there is simply a recognition that they have a role to play in the circumstances as they are. If the circumstances need to be different, so does the meaning making they have applied to get there.

Peers

The three key stages within this dimension are: **defined, chosen,** and **re-formed**. In the *defined* stage, the client does not recognize they have any choice in who they see as peers, and as a result, play a similar role in all the groups they work in or belong to. The client does not believe they have any control in the creation of their peer groups or who might belong in them, are unable to determine dynamically what role they could play in peer groups, and simply do not know how to interact with peers. They assume all peer groups as fixed and therefore their role and behaviours within these groups as equally fixed.

The sense of agency and choice that clients feel in the next stage of *chosen* is dramatically different. The client realizes they can have agency over their perception of the peer groups and, as a result, will feel then can choose to connect and belong or to hold themselves apart. This new feeling of agency extends beyond belonging. The client can feel that they are able to choose which role they want to play within these different peer groups. In addition, they know they can learn from and deal with peer groups that they do not identify with or enjoy associating with.

The final stage is *re-formed*, in which the needs of others, versus the needs of the client, drive the association into different groups. The client is able to respond and react based on their current context and the needs of others and therefore also have significant flexibility in what role to play in these groups. These groups and the roles the client plays within them change constantly, again based on the current context of needs of others and sits agnostic from what the client needs for themself. Importantly, clients may find that they do not always need to associate with any peer groups at all, but can also derive deep pleasure and value when required or when they desire to be part of a group. With the support and connection of peers becoming less necessary, the peer groups to which a client might belong is a less well-formed peer group.

Identity

The three key stages within this dimension are: **inherited, constructed,** and **transformative**. *Inherited* is the sense the client has that identity imposed upon them. They have no choice in deciding who they are supposed to be. Who they are supposed to be has been decided by their family of origin, or what the culture, religion, race, societal expectations, or the organization itself has imposed on them. Some clients will feel great turmoil here as they are unable to shed the expectations of others, despite their own needs to stand apart from what was imposed on them. A client may feel deep alignment to who they were told to be and therefore struggle with any identity change, particularly if the context around them requires it.

In the *constructed* stage, the client feels that they have a greater choice about who they want to be and how they want to define themself. They also feel they have the right to experiment with their identity, to try on different selves, so to speak. This stage can feel very static for the client in that once they have made the choice to shift or change aspects of their identity, they are often very unwilling to move or sacrifice for the sake of the greater good. They are unapologetically who they are in this constructed stage and will feel a great deal of turmoil if anyone challenges or imposes upon them anything that does not align with who they want to be.

In the final *transformative* stage, identity becomes an unnecessary label. There is always a sense of self, but it is not a static identity but more of an energy field in constant motion. Identity becomes something more emergent based on what is happening around them. There is a deep sense of comfort in who they are, with a high degree of self-awareness. But this sense of identity is no longer an essential aspect of knowing required by the client. They can take on different facets of identity and can learn from different ways of being. They can flex who they are while remaining steadfast in the certainty of their own knowingness of themselves. The client in this phase will also be constantly experimenting with different ways of being, identifying, and interacting with the world, and find that the dance or emergence into something new and unknown is the core goal.

Context

The three key stages within this dimension are: **fixed, explored,** and **emergent**. In the *fixed* stage, the context of the client's life remains fundamentally unchanged; that is, the circumstances in which the client was raised continues to be the defining characteristics of their lives. Often, these clients maintain the status quo because they either don't want change, or have never had the need to question their context and therefore prefer to stay within the comfort of the familiar. In some cases, it is simply not possible to change. Whatever the reason, the circumstances under which the client was born and raised define how they see the world and themselves within it.

Clients in the *explored* stage are more curious, looking to experience different contexts from the one in which they were raised. They also feel they have the agency to choose the context that reflects their evolving values as an adult. These are often clients who have chosen to live in different countries than the one of birth and often travel extensively in order to submerse themselves in the different. They seek differences as a way of experimenting with their own belief systems and context.

The *emergent* stage is the third stage, and as in other dimensions, this third stage is characterized by unfettered exploration and independence as clients no longer feel the need to classify or self-identify with a category or group. Clients in this stage do not depend on a socioeconomic, religious, or cultural identity to fill in their context. Even race is not central to their identity, although it might offer a perspective for reflection. Clients in this third stage are multi-faceted. In some cases, these clients can often have deep associations within multiple groups and easily find connection and belonging to others. Meanwhile other clients may be almost oblivious to connection and live fully self-sufficient lives.

Emotional Spectrum

The three key stages within this dimension are: **controlled, optimized,** and **indicator**. In the *controlled* stage, the client feels that emotions are uncontrollable or are meant to be totally controlled. The clients in this stage are often raised in households of one of two extremes: either emotions were expressed without filters or thought, regardless of the impact of such expression, or emotions were completely suppressed. As adults, these clients cannot manage their emotions, but instead indulge or suppress emotions that they feel are too much to deal with. Some do not hesitate to express escape emotions, such as anger and fear, in order to release and externalize what is happening to them, but find attachment-based emotions, such as love and joy, inaccessible and/or inexpressible. Others will find suppression of all emotions as the safest option as they themselves do not have the capacity to understand what is really happening within them.

As the client moves into the *optimized* stage, they recognize that emotions are indicators of things that lie deep within the non-conscious. They also focus in this stage on attachment-based emotions, such as love and joy, which they seek to make prevalent in their lives. However, emotions are also to be managed, especially to avoid negatively impacting others. For that reason, escape emotions, such as anger and sadness, are more likely to be suppressed.

For the client in the third *indicator* stage, the attachment emotions of love and joy are more than prevalent, they permeate through every experience, action, and reaction to others. These clients are not afraid to explore the deeper escape emotions of sadness, shame, and fear, seeking to shine a light on what sits in the non-conscious behind those emotions. Emotions thus act as a barometer of deeper self-awareness, rather than an expression. Clients in this stage also have a tremendous capacity to connect with others easily as their own need for emotional management is inconsequential.

Relationship

The three key stages within this dimension are: **dependent, dynamic,** and **love**. The first stage is the *dependent* stage–a stage, in psychological terms, characterized by insecure attachment. Often because of past trauma in their childhood years, the client in this stage may be afraid of either being abandoned or being locked into relationships defined by constraints. As a result, they find it difficult to develop relationships with others based on healthy levels of autonomy.

In contrast, clients in the second stage, the *dynamic* stage, are able to develop relationships with healthy boundaries. They are also able to break free of the familiar and develop different types of relationships and experiment with being in relationships with different types of people. They also find themselves stretching the boundaries of the forms of relationship that can exist. Second stage clients are not always secure in their relationships, but even then, there is a greater awareness of the need for secured attachments.

The third stage of relationships is simply called *love*, for it is indeed characterized by an overwhelming desire for love in all relationships. In this stage, the clients are less focused on any single relationship but seek instead a general connection to love around them. The unfortunate by-product of this focus on love for all is the potential neglect of what is typically called 'loved ones'–that is, the people closest to the clients. As the saying goes: a friend to all but a lover to none!

Does the Coach's Stage Matter?

We have focused in this chapter on the stages of the clients. However, the coaches are themselves in one of the three stages for each of these dimensions. What happens if a client is in a later stage of development than a coach? What happens, for example, if a coach is in the first, dependent stage of the emotional spectrum, while the client has already moved on to the second stage, optimize. In this case, according to one of the principles of the constructive-developmental approach, it is less likely the coach would be able to act as a reflective partner for the client. (Bachkirova, 2014). That is why nearly a third of the interviewees urged coaches to do 'our own work' before setting out to do work with others. Until coaches can resolve their own significant traumas in their own biographical history, it is unlikely they will be able to help their clients with their issues. *'We have to start on ourselves,'* explained one interviewee. *'If we haven't done the work, processed and healed, we cannot partner with our clients to do a version of the same. It will be too dangerous for us both.'*

Exploring Trauma and its Impact on Stages

Foundational to all work related to the past, is the notion of trauma. It is important to first define what is trauma and how to identify it when working with clients. I define trauma as an *emotional response* to a distressing experience. Trauma can *undermine a client's sense of safety* or infringe upon an *individual's sense of control*. It may *reduce their capacity to integrate* the situation or circumstances into their current reality.

Equally, it is important to note not all trauma is the same. There what is referred to as big 'T' trauma, defined as deeply disturbing event(s) that have a profound and at times debilitating impact on the individual. These types of traumas can include acute trauma, chronic trauma, and adverse child experiences (ACE). Acute trauma is characterized by a sudden event, outside the control of the client, that has profound impact on the client. Common examples include a car crash, physical or sexual assault[1], or the sudden death

---

[1] For definitions of these terms, reference to the magazine Psychology Today's glossary is valuable: https://www.psychologytoday.com/gb/basics

of a loved one. Chronic trauma often arises from harmful events that are repeated or prolonged. It can develop in response to persistent bullying, neglect, abuse (emotional, physical, or sexual), and domestic violence. And finally adverse child experience is the profound trauma that young children are exposed to from a young age and often chronic in nature. The loss of a parent; neglect; emotional, physical, or sexual abuse; and divorce are among the most common.

On the other hand, we have what is called little 't' trauma, which is an accumulation of smaller or less pronounced events that may not cause post-traumatic stress syndrome, but still cause some degree of distress. This distress causes maladaptive coping mechanisms adopted to suppress or cope with the experience.

Regardless of the typology of the trauma, what is important to know in coaching is if there is a presence of a maladaptive coping strategies as a result of the trauma. In other words, we need an *understanding of the presence* of past trauma, its *current effects and impact* on a client (e.g. the adaptive strategies the client holds as a result of this trauma), and how to *use the client's resilience* to guide them along a path towards focused growth. If the client is still very much subject to the trauma, then coaching is not advisable. Creating space for the client to work on healing is the first step towards greater agency, and that healing in my opinion sits outside the goals of coaching in organizational environments.

Another essential aspect of working with trauma is how we contract as coaches. I have created a brief checklist for coaches to consider in how to make these agreements with their clients.

1. Create **safety** for your client and yourself. As mentioned before, as the coach, you need to have done this work on yourself in order to support others through their own journeys. Make sure you are safe and well-resourced for this work. Then make sure your client is well-resourced and able to do this work as well.
2. Create **clarity of task**, and interpersonal and professional boundaries. Define what is considered in-scope and out-of-scope and, together, make those calls in real-time. If the need for external support through counselling or therapy is required, you have a clearly defined process about how to handle this and have a list of resources for your client to lean on.
3. Empower client with **voice and choice** to have control over experience. The client must always be in the driver's seat on any exploration of the past. Your role as

coach is to offer the client exploration, support with correlation, and formulations. However, the client must have full and total decision-making on where they go, how deep they go, and what they do with these insights once discovered. Only the client can identify their stage within each dimension and when they are ready to do some integration work to get to the next stage.
4. Hold space with **empathy and mindfulness.** This is important and delicate work, so be sure to approach it with extreme empathy and mindfulness at all times.
5. **Seek support.** The essence of supervision when doing this type of work cannot be understated. As a coach, you will constantly be running up against what is yours, what is your client's, and what is existing in the space between you and client. Having an objective and well-resourced supervisor to support you in this important work is foundational.

Finally, when dealing with trauma, and this applies to any work that explores the past, it is important to consider both the resourcing and functioning of the client. The resourcing of the client is about their ability to self-regulate and be equipped with the tools required to do the important integration work of coaching. The other consideration is the functioning of the client. Is the client operating at sufficient levels in all their roles that if they begin discovery into areas that may cause some degree of disintegration or pain, that they can still operate in all the roles that are required of them? Ideally, we only work with clients who have a high degree of resourcing and functioning.

CHAPTER 8

Conclusions

At the heart of this book was the desire to shed light on the limited secondary research and almost non-existent empirically validated tools available to coaches in exploring the past with their clients. The main objective was to share the first evidenced-based framework of exploring the past with clients through BDMM© and helping coaches understand both the depth of the exploration and how those insights mapped to leadership tendencies in organizations. The unintended consequence of the research this book was based on was a more existential exploration of the nature of coaching and defining coaching within the realm of a third generation, and maybe even introducing the beginnings of a fourth-generation approach.

In addition, the original research this book was based on continues to grow and expand as this knowledge is rolled out to more and more coaching communities. It continues to build as I grow the number of certified BDMM© practitioners through the credentialing program. It is morphing into a more expansive field of application as I supervise coaches who are bringing their own approach to this work through their own practices. As I sit with this growth and overwhelming appreciation for how it is being received all over the world, I can't help but to keep thinking about the wisdom shared by Annette Fillery-Travis and Sarah

Corrie on the lagging pace of research due to the lack of collaboration between practitioners and academics in coaching (Fillery-Travis and Corrie, 2019).

So, I want to end this book where my new focus begins–on what's next for our industry and the shared responsibility we all hold in continuing to grow and build the field of coaching in both its research base, its regulation, and its growing application across the globe. This chapter will cover:

1. Pushing the boundaries of what the coaching industry could be.
2. Expanding the field of Coaching Psychology.
3. Creating a more inclusive approach to research and empirical application.

Pushing the Boundaries of What the Coaching Industry Could Be

As described earlier in Chapter 4, the field of coaching is growing at breakneck speed. With an estimated industry revenue size of US$4.5Bn, coaching is considered the second fastest-growing global sector with more than 109,000 coaches worldwide (PWC, 2022). With this speed of growth comes an explosion of coaching philosophies–some of them rooted in psychology and applied sciences while others are creating movement towards spirituality and more Eastern-centric philosophies. As the industry expands, so too does the need for better oversight, governance, and the building of an empirical research basis.

The challenges we face in the coaching industry in some ways all come down to a single issue: do we want a global standardization of who we are, what we do, and how we govern ourselves? There is much debate around this issue, compounded by the fact that we have grown in large part by inviting practitioners from other fields into a space that feels more expansive and less regulated than their previous professional homes. Further complicating the issue is the relatively low barriers to entry into this profession, where a few days of training can now qualify you as being a 'certified coach'. It is this speed of growth and the lack of unity around what defines us that is creating real challenges on defining what the work of coaching really is.

Instead of creating global industry standards, we are allowing the largest professional coaching bodies to do the defining for us. The International Coaching Federation (ICF) being the kingpin in this field is now being challenged by other organizations such as the European Mentoring and Coaching Council (EMCC), the International Association of Coaching (IAC), and Association for Coaching (AC). Having gratefully been invited into some of these communities to speak about BDMM©, what I am noticing is more and more fractionalization instead of unification towards global definitions.

While this may be the natural course of progression for any growing field of practice, there are some fundamental ethical concerns that are emerging. I have now done more than 50 keynote addresses to various coaching communities (both large and small) across three continents in the past five years. I open all my talks with the same question: 'Does the past matter in coaching?' Five years ago, the room was often divided at almost 50/50. Now, the response is the vast majority of people will say, 'Yes, it matters'. My next question would be, 'How many of you have had some form of professional psychological training to do that type of work?' The response was often less than 20% of the room. My conclusion: people are doing this work but have no training in how to ethically hold these conversations. So, what has been our response as a coaching profession? Organizations like the ICF state in their core competencies that any work related to the past is considered counselling or therapy and therefore outside the scope of coaching. Simply put, I believe this is an unacceptable approach.

My suggestion is that an industry-wide effort

(agnostic of any professional coaching body) needs to be made to better identify and define what is coaching and how can different schools of thought exist within it. My particular interest is in the use of biographical inquiry (BI) in executive coaching. As described earlier in the book, uncovering relevant bodies of research was challenging, exhausting, and often futile. Coaching begins with a person who has a history, so why then do we not have more coaching research related to working with those histories?

Additionally, professional coaching bodies need to provide more explicit guidelines and suggestions related to the transitions between stages and/or coaching credentials. The need is especially acute for mid-to-senior coaches who often are left feeling underwhelmed by the quality of dialogue and professional engagement around complex issues in coaching. Most of these seasoned coaches then find their 'professional homes' outside these major coaching bodies and rarely venture beyond their fields of interest. As such, we never really engage in the essential professional debate that needs to happen when diverse and often conflicting views come to be discussed on the issues that really matter to the community as a whole. These bodies need to move away from focusing only on how they commercialize their communities by offering different credentialling pathways to actually focusing on what is working and broken in the profession overall.

Expanding the field of Coaching Psychology

I believe the emergence of the field of coaching psychology is a movement in the right direction towards the professionalization of coaching. Yet Grant (2011) suggested that even within the coaching psychology communities, without a clear definition, the field of coaching psychology could not be fully developed and properly taught. A unifying definition is needed to help move the field of coaching psychology forward.

As one of these seasoned coaches who became disillusioned with the large professional coaching bodies, I found kinship in the field of coaching psychology. A field that was more focused on social–psychological perspectives (Passmore and Lai, 2020), it had the best quality research, and was engaging in the difficult but important discussions around regulation, mandatory supervision, and creating multiple pathways for specialization. I proudly call myself a coaching psychologist, this book is a *coaching psychology* book, and most of my professional mentors belong to this field within coaching. But, we still have some major challenges.

Firstly, the research in coaching psychology is dropping, not growing. In a systematic review of all coaching psychology research between 2010 and 2016, Lai and Palmer (2019) found that the total number of external papers dropped from 141 in 2010 to 113 in 2016. Secondly, the vast majority of psychologically based research is in cognitive-behavioural coaching and solutions-focused coaching with a rise in strengths-based coaching, creating a real gap in the psychodynamic and psychotherapeutic approaches. Third, membership in this community is primarily driven by psychologists who have become coaches versus the other way around–making diversity of thought challenging. Lastly, we suffer greatly from a general lack of diversity in both research practitioners and where these research studies are taking place. When doing my research for my doctorate, there was not one single research study that was based outside of the US, UK/Europe, or Australia.

My hope is that we can grow this field by generating research that does not simply borrow from psychology or use psychological informed approaches but creates our own theoretical approaches, which I believe is what BDMM© offers.

Creating a More Inclusive Approach to Research and Empirical Application

I naively thought completing my doctorate would be the hardest part of the journey. What I discovered was disseminating the information into the world was in fact the real challenge. Finding ways to bring this knowledge to various communities, and finding opportunities to publish and share insights and, fundamentally, to influence change on both an industry and global basis is a never-ending mission.

I was blessed that I had a rich network of professional coaches who brought me into their communities. I had clients who were bravely willing to take a risk and bring these evocative ideas into their organizations. And finally, I had access to powerful platforms that allowed me to publish my ideas with the world. Where I have been most disappointed is in the academic institutions and academic journals due to their very restrictive views on how to disseminate information.

While universities are trying to create professional doctorate pathways for practitioners, they give little to no support in helping their students get published in renowned academic journals so that their ideas can get better disseminated in the world.

Furthermore, the academic journals themselves, while robust in their vetting process of eligibility and unrelenting in their standards of writing, make it almost impossible for practitioner-scholars to actually publish their work. Without the knowledge and support of tenured academic scholars who mentor and /or co-write these articles, most practitioner-scholars have little chance of ever having their work considered. At the centre of the issue, in my opinion, is that academic journals are targeted at scholars who frankly, only want to hear from other scholars. What is the value in creating practitioner-scholar pathways in universities if the research stemming from these theses are never shared in the academic world? In my view, most practitioner-scholars focus almost exclusively on the private sector, because the barriers are substantively lower. How will we ever really move the industry forward if we keep losing our practitioner-scholars to the private sector?

Finally, more diversity needs to be built into coaching research. Most, if not all, of the major post-graduate coaching programmes are in English and based and delivered almost entirely in a Western-centric context. These programmes should make an effort to involve more scholars, practitioners, and practitioner-scholars from more geographically diverse places. As noted

Conclusions

above, the barriers to entry into the field of academic writing are nearly insurmountable. A more concerted effort is needed by scholars, journal publishers, and universities to support these often non-English speakers and/or non-Western perspectives in becoming part of the collective consciousness of the coaching industry.

Final Thoughts

I am immensely proud of this book and the research I have produced. But what brings me more joy and ultimately purpose is watching how other coaches are adopting this work in their own ways in service of their own purpose-driven missions. I hope my work can spark a flame in others to continue to build on the work of BI in coaching. This book contains the beginnings of a new language. As the users of this language grow and evolve, so too will the language itself. My ask is to please share your voice with the world. We need more practitioner-scholars in this field to help us grow our knowledge base, but more importantly, to further professionalize the industry of coaching.

My wish is that anyone who comes across this book will feel challenged and curious about what can be inferred. My hope is that such feelings of challenge or curiosity will grow into a desire to contribute further research in our industry, so we can collectively rise, together.

Further Reading

Further Reading

1. Aquilina, E. and Strozzi-Heckler, R. (2019) 'Somatic Coaching', in Palmer, S. and Whybrow, A. (eds.) *Handbook of Coaching Psychology: A Guide for Practitioners*. 2nd edn. Adingdon: Routledge, pp. 229-240.
2. Aunola, K., Stattin, H. and Nurmi, J.-E. (2000) 'Parenting styles and adolescents' achievement strategies', *Journal of Adolescence*, 23(2), pp. 205-222. doi: 10.1006/jado.2000.0308
3. Bachkirova, T. (2011). *Developmental Coaching: Working with the Self*. Maidenhead: Open University Press.
4. Bachkirova, T. (2014) 'Psychological Development in Adulthood and Coaching', in Cox, E., Bachkirova, T. and Clutterbuck, D. (eds.) *The Complete Handbook of Coaching*. 2nd edn. London: Sage Publications, pp. 131-144.
5. Bachkirova, T. and Barker, S. (2019) 'Revisiting the issue of boundaries between coaching and counselling', in Palmer, S. and Whybrow, A. (eds.) *Handbook of Coaching Psychology: A Guide for Practitioners*. 2nd edn. Abingdon: Routledge, pp. 487-499.
6. Bachkirova, T. and Cox, E. (2007) 'Coaching with emotion in organisations: Investigation of personal theories', *Leadership & Organization Development Journal*, 28(7), pp. 600-612. doi: 10.1108/01437730710823860
7. Berger, J.G. (2012) 'Using the subject-object interview to promote and assess self-authorship', in Magolda, M.B.B., Meszaros P.S. and Creamer, E.G.

(eds.) *Development and Assessment of Self-Authorship: Exploring the Concept Across Cultures*. Sterling: Stylus Publishing, pp. 245-264.

8. Brown, P. and Brown, V. (2012). *Neuropsychology for Coaches: Understanding the Basics.* London: Open University Press.

9. Brown, P. T. and Dzendrowskyj, T. (2018) 'Sorting Out an Emotional Muddle: insights from neuroscience on the organizational value of emotions', *Developing Leaders*, Issue 29, pp. 26-31.

10. Bush, M.W., Ozkan, E. and Passmore, J. (2012) 'The development of meaning and identity within coaching', in Passmore, J., Peterson, D. B. and Freire, T. (eds.) *The Wiley-Blackwell Handbook of the Psychology of Coaching and Mentoring.* Hoboken: Wiley-Blackwell, pp. 58-67.

11. Cook-Greuter, S. (1985) *A detailed description of the successive stages in ego development theory*, Paper presented at the second annual meeting of the Society for Research in Adult Development, Cambridge, MA.

12. Cunningham, N. (2017) 'Coaching: Meaning-making process or goal-resolution process?', *Philosophy of Coaching: An International Journal*, 2(2), pp. 83-101. doi: 10.22316/poc/02.2.06

13. Cushion, C. (2015) 'Reflection and reflective practice discourses in coaching: a critical analysis', *Sport, Education and Society*, 23(1), pp. 82-94. doi: 10.1080/13573322.2016.1142961

14. Day, A., Haan, E., Sills, C., Bertie, C. and Blass, E. (2008) 'Coaches' experience of critical moments

in the coaching', *International Coaching Psychology Review*, 3(3), pp. 207-218.

15. Dodwell, T. (2020) 'Coaching approaches for a lost sense of self - hunt it down or let it be?', *The Coaching Psychologist*, 16(1), pp. 11.

16. Drake, D. (2016) 'Working with narratives in coaching', in Bachkirova, T., Spence, G. and Drake, D. (eds.) *The SAGE Handbook of Coaching*. London: Sage Publications, pp. 291-309.

17. Drake, D.B. (2009) 'Using attachment theory in coaching leaders: The search for a coherent narrative', *International Coaching Psychology Review*, 4(1), pp. 49-58.

18. Eigel, K.M., and Kuhnert, K.W. (2005) 'Authentic development: Leadership development level and executive effectiveness', in Garner, W. Avioloi, B and Walumba, F. (eds.) *Perspectives on Authentic Leadership Development*. New York: Elsevier Press, pp. 357-385.

19. Ellis, C., Adams, T. and Bochner, A. (2011) 'Autoethnography: An Overview', *Historical Social Research / Historische Sozialforschung*, 36(4), pp. 273-290.

20. Erikson, E.(1950). *Childhood and of the Society*. New York: Norton.

21. Fillery-Travis, A. and Corrie, S. (2019) 'Research and the practitioner: getting a perspective on evidence as a coaching psychologist', in Palmer, S. and Whybrow, A. (eds.) *Handbook of Coaching Psychology: A Guide for Practitioners*. 2nd edn. Abingdon: Routledge, pp. 68-79.

22. Frankl, V. (1946). *Man's Search for Meaning*. Boston: Beacon Press.
23. Glasgow, K.L., Dornbusch, S.M., Troyer, L., Steinberg, L. and Ritter, P.L. (1997) 'Parenting styles, adolescents' attributions, and educational outcomes in nine heterogeneous high schools', *Child Development*, 68(3), pp. 507-529.
24. Graci, M.E. and Fivush, R. (2017) 'Narrative meaning making, attachment, and psychological growth and stress', *Journal of Social and Personal Relationships*, 34(4), pp. 486-509. doi: 10.1177/0265407516644066
25. Grant, A.M. (2011) 'Developing an agenda for teaching coaching psychology', *International Coaching Psychology Review*, 6(1), pp. 84-99.
26. Grant, A.M. (2016) 'The third 'generation' of workplace coaching: creating a culture of quality conversations', *Coaching: An International Journal of Theory, Research and Practice*, 10(1), pp. 37-53. doi: 10.1080/17521882.2016.1266005
27. Grimley, B. (2019) 'Neuro Linguistic Programming (NLP) and coaching', in Palmer, S. and Whybrow, A. (eds.) *Handbook of Coaching Psychology: A Guide for Practitioners*. 2nd edn. Abingdon: Routledge, pp. 282-294.
28. Gus, L., Rose, J. and Gilbert, L. (2015) 'Emotion Coaching, a universal strategy for supporting and promoting sustainable emotional and behavioural well-being', *Educational and Child Psychology*, 32(1), pp. 31-41.
29. Habermas, T. (2011) 'Autobiographical reasoning:

Arguing and narrating from a biographical perspective', *New Directions for Child and Adolescent Development*, 131, pp. 1-17.

30. Hasanie, S. (2019) 'Conscious and Non-Conscious Meaning Making', *International Coaching Federation - Singapore Chapter Event*, Monday 25 November.

31. Hébert, C. (2015) 'Knowing and/or experiencing: a critical examination of the reflective models of John Dewey and Donald Schön', *Reflective Practice*, 16(3), pp. 361-371. doi: 10.1080/14623943.2015.1023281

32. Hemming, M.E., Blackmer, V. and Searight, R.H. (2012) 'The Family-of-Origin Scale: A Psychometric Review and Factor Analytic Study', *International Journal of Psychological Studies*, 4(3), pp. 34-42. doi: 10.5539/ijps.v4n3p34

33. Hemmings, B. (2012) 'Sources of research confidence for early career academics: a qualitative study', *Higher Education Research & Development*, 31(2), pp. 171-184. doi: 10.1080/07294360.2011.559198

34. Hovestadt, A.J., Anderson, W. T., Piercy, F.P., Cochran, S.W. and Fine, M. (1985) 'A Family-Of-Origin Scale', *Journal of Marital and Family Therapy*, 11(3), pp. 287-297. doi: 10.1111/j.1752-0606.1985.tb00621.x

35. International Coaching Federation. (2009) *ICF Global Coaching Client Study 2006*, Available at: *https://researchportal.coachfederation.org/Document/Pdf/abstract_190*.

36. International Coaching Federation. (2016) *2016 ICF*

Global Coaching Study, Available at: *https://coachingfederation.org/research/global-coaching-study*.

37. Ives, R. (2008) 'What is 'Coaching'? An Exploration of Conflicting Paradigms', *International Journal of Evidence Based Coaching and Mentoring*, 6(2), pp. 100-113.

38. Kegan, R. (1982). *The Evolving Self: Problem and Process in Human Development*. Cambridge, Mass: Harvard University Press.

39. Kegan, R. (1994). *In Over Our Heads*. Cambridge, Mass: Harvard University Press.

40. Keller, T. (1999) 'Images of the familiar: Individual differences and implicit leadership theories', *The Leadership Quarterly*, 10(4), pp. 589-607.

41. Keller, T. (2003) 'Parental images as a guide to leadership sensemaking: An attachment perspective on implicit leadership theories', *The Leadership Quarterly*, 14(2), pp. 141-160. doi: 10.1016/S1048-9843(03)00007-9

42. Kempster, S. and Iszatt-White, M. (2013) 'Towards co-constructed coaching: exploring the integration of coaching and co-constructed autoethnography in leadership development', *Management Learning*, 44(4), pp. 319-336. doi: 10.1177/1350507612449959

43. Kovacs, L. and Corrie, S,. (2021) 'Formulation as a foundation for navigating complexity in executive coaching', *Consulting Psychology: Practice & Research*, 73(3), pp. 271-288. doi: 10.1037/cpb0000202

44. Lai, Y.L. and Palmer, S. (2019) 'Understanding

evidence-based coaching through the analysis of coaching methodology', in Palmer, S. and Whybrow, A. (eds.) *Handbook of Coaching Psychology: A Guide for Practitioners*. 2nd edn. Abingdon: Routledge, pp. 80-90.

45. Lane, D. and Corrie, S. (2009) 'Does Coaching Psychology Need the Concept of Formulation?', *International Coaching Psychology Review*, 4(2), pp. 103-206.

46. Lawrence, P. (2016) 'Coaching and Adult Development', in Bachkirova, T., Spence, G. and Drake, D. (eds.) *The SAGE Handbook for Coaching*. London: Sage Publications, pp. 121-138.

47. Leifman, H.D. (2001). *Family of Origin Roles and Adult Work Roles in Relation to Employee Adjustment, Satisfaction and Success*. New York: ProQuest Dissertations Publishing.

48. Loevinger, J. (1979) 'The Idea of the Ego', *The Counseling Psychologist*, 8(2), pp. 3-5. doi: 10.1177/001100007900800202

49. Magomaeva, A. (2013) *"Who Taught Us How to Lead?" Parental Influence On Leadership Styles*, Thesis for M.A in Psychology, Wayne State University. https://digitalcommons.wayne.edu/oa_theses/307

50. Manning, T.T. (2003) 'Leadership Across Cultures: Attachment Style Influences', *Journal of Leadership & Organizational Studies*, 9(3), pp. 20-30. doi: 10.1177/107179190300900304

51. Mayseless, O. (2010) 'Attachment and the leader-follower relationship', *Journal of Social and Personal Relationships*, 27(2), pp. 271-280. doi: 10.1177/0265407509360904

52. McAdams, D.P. (2018) 'Narrative Identity: What Is It? What Does It Do? How Do You Measure It?', *Imagination, Cognition and Personality*, 37(3), pp. 359-372. doi: 10.1177/0276236618756704

53. Merron, K., Fisher, D. and Torbert, W.R. (1987) 'Meaning Making and Management Action', *Group & Organization Management*, 12(3), pp. 274-286. doi: 10.1177/105960118701200304

54. Mumford, M.D., O'Connor, J., Clifton, T.C., Connelly, M.S. and Zaccaro, S.J. (2009) 'Background Data Constructs as Predictors of leadership', *Human Performance*, 6(2), pp. 151-195. doi: 10.1207/s15327043hup0602_4

55. O'Broin, A. and Palmer, S. (2019) 'The coaching relationship: a key role in coaching processes and outcomes', in Palmer, S. and Whybrow, A. (eds.) *Handbook of Coaching Psychology: A Guide for Practitioners*. 2nd edn. Abingdon: Routledge, pp. 471-486.

56. Oakley, D. and Halligan, P. (2017) 'Chasing the rainbow: The non-conscious nature of being', *Frontiers in Psychology*, 8, Article 1924. doi: 10.3389/fpsyg.2017.01924

57. Passmore, J. (2010) 'Diversity in Coaching: Working with Gender, Culture, Race and Age', *Human Resource Management International Digest*, 18 (2). doi: 10.1108/hrmid.2010.04418bae.002

58. Passmore, J. and Fillery-travis, A. (2011) 'A critical review of executive coaching research: A decade of progress and what's to come', *Coaching An International Journal of Theory Research and Practice*, 4(2),

pp. 70-88. doi: 10.1080/17521882.2011.596484
59. Passmore, J. and Lai, Y.L. (2020) 'Coaching Psychology: Exploring Definitions and Research Contribution to Practice', in Passmore, J. and Tee, D. (eds.) *Coaching Researched: A Coaching Psychology Reader.* Hoboken: John Wiley and Sons, pp. 3-22.
60. Piaget, J. (1971). *Psychology and Epistemology: Towards a Theory of Knowledge.* New York: Grossman.
61. Pillemer, D.B. (1998). *Momentous Events, Vivid Memories.* Cambridge, Mass: Harvard University Press.
62. Pillemer, D.B. (2001) 'Momentous Events and the Life Story', *Review of General Psychology*, 5(2), pp. 123-134. doi: 10.1037/1089-2680.5.2.123
63. Pillemer, D.B., Krensky, L., Kleinman, S.N., Goldsmith, L.R. and White, S.H. (1991) 'Chapters in Narratives: Evidence From Oral Histories of the First Year in College', *Journal of Narrative and Life History*, 1(1), pp. 3-14.
64. Praskova, A. and Johnston, L. (2021) 'The Role of Future Orientation and Negative Career Feedback in Career Agency and Career Success in Australian Adults', *Journal of Career Assessment*, 29(3), pp. 463-485. doi: 10.1177/1069072720980174
65. PWC (2023) ICF Global Coa0ching Study; https://coachingfederation.org/research/global-coaching-study
66. Rankin-Wright, A., Hylton, K. and Norman, L. (2017) 'Negotiating the coaching landscape: Experiences of Black men and women coaches in

the United Kingdom', *International Review for the Sociology of Sport*, 54(5), pp. 603-621. doi: 10.1177/1012690217724879

67. Roberts, V.Z. and Brunning, H. (2019) 'Psychodynamic and systems-psychodynamic coaching', in Palmer, S. and Whybrow, A. (eds.) *Handbook of Coaching Psychology: A Guide for Practitioners.* 2nd edn. Abingdon: Routledge, pp. 324-340.

68. Rosinski, P. (2011) 'Global Coaching for Organizational Development', *IJCO International Journal of Coaching in Organizations*, Issue 30, 8(2), pp. 49-66.

69. Roth, A. (2017) 'Coaching a client with a different cultural background - does it matter?', *International Journal of Evidence Based Coaching and Mentoring*, Special Issue No.11, pp. 30-43.

70. Rothaizer, J.M. and Hill, S.L. (2009) 'Coaching and the Unconscious', *International Journal of Coaching in Organizations,* 7(3), pp. 55-72.

71. Rubin, D.C., Rahhal, A. and Poon, L.W. (1998) 'Things learned in early adulthood are remembered best', *Memory & Cognition*, 26(1), pp. 3-19. doi: 10.3758/bf03211366

72. Rutten, K. and Flory, M. (2020) 'Managing meanings, coaching virtues and mediating rhetoric: Revisiting the role of rhetoric and narratives in management research and practice', *Journal of Organizational Change Management*, 33(4), pp. 581-590. doi: 10.1108/JOCM-11-2019-0333

73. Sexton, T.L. (1997) 'Constructivist thinking within the history of ideas: The challenge of a new para-

digm', in Sexton, T.L. and Griffin, B. L. (eds.) *Constructivist Thinking in Counseling Practice Research and Training.* New York: Teachers College Press, pp. 3-18.

74. Shiemann, S.J, Muhlberger, C., Schoorman, D.F. and Jonas, E. (2019) 'Trust me, I am a caring coach: The benefits of establishing trustworthiness during coaching by communicating benevolence', *Journal of Trust Research,* 9(2), pp. 164-184. doi: 10.1080/21515581.2019.1650751

75. Stelter, R. (2007) 'Coaching: A process of personal and social meaning making', *International Coaching Psychology Review,* 2(2), pp. 191-201.

76. Stelter, R. (2014) 'Third-generation coaching– striving towards value-oriented and collaborative dialogues', *International Coaching Psychology Review,* 9(1), pp. 51-66.

77. Strang, S.E. and Kuhnert, K.W. (2009) 'Personality and Leadership Developmental Levels as predictors of leader performance', *The Leadership Quarterly,* 20(3), pp. 421-433. doi: 10.1016/j.leaqua.2009.03.009

78. Strozzi-Heckler, R. (2014). *The Art of Somatic Coaching: Embodying Skillful Action, Wisdom, and Compassion.* Berkeley: North Atlantic Books.

79. Tudge, J. and Rogoff, B., (1999) 'Peer influences on cognitive development: Piagetian and Vygotskian perspectives', in Lloyd, P. and Fernyhough, C. (eds.) *Lev Vygotsky: critical assessments.* Vol. 3. London: Routledge, pp. 32-56.

80. Vogel, M. (2012) 'Story Matters: An Inquiry into the

Role of Narrative in Coaching', *International Journal of Evidence Based Coaching and Mentoring*, 10(1), pp. 1-10.
81. Vygotsky, L.S.(1978). *Mind in Society: The Development of Higher Psychological Processes.* Cambridge, Mass: Harvard University Press.
82. Wilbur, K. (1999) 'Spirituality and developmental lines: are there stages?', *The Journal of Transpersonal Psychology*, 31(1), pp. 1-10.
83. Wilson, T.D. (2004). *Strangers to Ourselves: Discovering the Adaptive Unconscious.* Cambridge, Mass: Belknap Press.
84. Zheng, L, Lippke, S., Chen, D.L., Li, D. and Gan, Y. (2019) 'Future orientation buffers depression in daily and specific stress', *PsyCH Journal*, 8(3), pp. 342-352. doi: 10.1002/pchj.283

Hasanie, S. (2020a) 'A Neuroscience Based Model of Exploration with Clients – How to Explore Conscious and Non–Conscious Meaning Making', Center for Creative Leadership in Singapore - Community of Practise Event, Thursday 13 February.

Hasanie, S. (2020b) 'Leadership in Times of Complexity - Using Psychology and Applied Neuroscience to aid with meaning making', Leadership Webinar Series for Civil Service College in Singapore, Wednesday 28 October.

Hasanie, S. (2020c) 'The Re-Imagination of Meaning Making in Organizations', Global TLC Conference, Thursday 29 October.

Hasanie, S. (2021a) 'Working with Reactive Tendencies - How Biographical Dimensions of Meaning Making can deepen your work with clients', The Leadership Circle Asia-Pacific Community of Practise, Thursday 29 April.

Hasanie, S. (2021b) 'Biographical Dimensions of Meaning Making', ION Meeting Community of Practice, Tuesday 1 June.

Hasanie, S. (2021c) 'Biographical Dimensions of Meaning Making', Singapore Psychological Association - Coaching Psychology Special Interest Group, Wednesday 25 August.

Hasanie, S. (2021d) 'Third Generation Coaching: The Journey to Shunya through the Acknowledgement,

Celebration and Nurturing of the Past, Present and Future', The Coaching Conclave Global Conference, Thursday 23 September.

Hasanie, S. (2021e) 'Working with Meaning Making through Vertical Development', Civil Service College of Singapore, Friday 1 October.

www.ingramcontent.com/pod-product-compliance
Lightning Source LLC
Chambersburg PA
CBHW040222040426
42333CB00050B/3292